BEARING
FRUIT

BEARING FRUIT

What
Happens When

God's People Grow

ROBBY GALLATY

PUBLISHING
NASHVILLE, TENNESSEE

Published by B&H Publishing Group
Nashville, Tennessee

Dewey Decimal Classification: 248.84
Subject Heading: CHRISTIAN LIFE \ DISCIPLESHIP \
FAITH

Cover design by B&H Publishing Group.
Icons by Aleksei_Derin/vectorstock.
Author photo by Jo McVey Photography LLC.

1 2 3 4 5 6 • 25 24 23 22

Book 1
Growing Up
Psalm 1:1–2

How happy is the one who does not walk in
the advice of the wicked or stand in the pathway
with sinners or sit in the company of mockers!
Instead, his delight is in the Lord's instruction,
and he meditates on it day and night.

Book 2
Firmly Planted
Psalm 1:3a

He is like a tree planted beside flowing streams . . .

Book 3
Bearing Fruit
Psalm 1:3b

. . . that bears its fruit in its season and whose
leaf does not wither. Whatever he does prospers.

To Chris Swain

No one I know lived out the principles
in this series more than you. You lived every
day with the end in mind. Your investment
in pastors, believers, friends, and family
will reverberate for years to come.

CONTENTS

FOREWORD

I love to read a good book that is both enlightening and convicting. As I dove into *Bearing Fruit*, I noticed that two things were happening before I could finish chapter 1. I was reading with much anticipation, but I was also praying in what I was reading. "Lord, make this truth a reality in my life. Oh God, may this fruit be produced by the Holy Spirit in my life. Let others consume this refreshment from my life." I could hardly wait for the next chapter. *Bearing Fruit* is a book that reminds us of the importance of the basics.

Do you ever find yourself knowing more than you are living? Knowledge over obedience? Then this is the book for you. If one word is too often absent in our Christian vocabulary, it is the word *works* or *fruit*. Fruit is the product of the Spirit of God at work in the life of the believer. Dr. Gallaty does an outstanding job of helping us to see what the Lord produces in our life as we yield to His Spirit. This fruit becomes that which the Lord uses to minister mightily in the life of other believers and unbelievers.

The author not only clearly explains the wonderful truths of abiding in Christ, but the results of this abiding. Read, pray, assimilate, and experience the change.

Johnny Hunt, vice president of Evangelism and
Leadership, North American Mission Board

INTRODUCTION

Every believer should be familiar with three theological words: *justification, sanctification,* and *glorification.* Justification is the act whereby God declares sinful human beings completely righteous and in right standing with God because they have received forgiveness from their sins through the death, burial, and resurrection of Jesus. A rudimentary way of thinking of it is "just as if I'd never sinned." You have been cleared of your transgressions and are now able to stand before a holy God.

Glorification is the future work of God, whereby he transforms our mortal bodies into our eternal bodies to dwell with him forever. When Jesus comes back, we will be made like him once and for all. Our corruptible bodies—as Paul stated in 1 Corinthians—will be incorruptible, and the mortal will put on immortality (1 Cor. 15:53). In essence, our faith will become sight as we overcome death, sin, suffering, crying, or pain.

In my opinion, sanctification is the most misunderstood concept of the three. Some have wrongly interpreted this to mean that God improves our unregenerate nature, or that he eradicates the old nature from us completely so we will never sin again. John Wesley wrongly taught sinless perfectionism, the idea that the Christian can become perfect in this life. A proper understanding of sanctification lies in a careful observation of the word itself. *Sanctify* is from the Greek word for "set apart" or "separate." God, throughout the Old and New Testaments, would sanctify a person, place, or thing to carry out his plans. For example, he sanctified a day in Genesis 2:3; he sanctified a building in 2 Chronicles 7:16; he sanctified a mountain in Exodus 19:23; and he sanctified himself in John 17:19. On what basis is the Christian sanctified? Hebrews 13:12 tells us, "Therefore, Jesus also suffered outside the gate, so that he might sanctify the people by his own blood." He offered his sinless body outside the gate so we can have access to God today. The finished work of Christ on the cross paved the way for a relationship with God.

Therefore, sanctification is the process whereby Christ lives his life through us. A distinction must be made between one's status before God and one's standing before God. "A person's status," according to theologian Herman Bavinck, "therefore, does not yet change his condition, nor vice versa. This holds true in the natural but also in the spiritual sphere. Sin is not merely guilt, but also pollution; we are delivered from the first by justification, from the second by sanctification."[1] **We could say that justification frees us from the penalty of sin, sanctification frees us from the power of sin, and glorification frees us from the presence of sin.**

Believers are expected to sanctify themselves in the Lord through the strength and power of the Spirit within each of us. We walk in the Spirit, as Paul instructed in Galatians 5:16, when we allow God to work *in* us and to work *through* us. The Christian life is either easy or impossible. It's impossible when we live it on our own strength. It becomes easier when we yield to God's rule and reign over our lives.

The entire process from start to finish is God's doing. A Christian can't grow himself; however, he can put himself in an environment for spiritual growth. When that happens, God brings forth fruit. In the parable of the sower and the seed, Jesus promised to produce fruit that yields one hundred, sixty, or thirty times what was sown. What kind of fruit grows in our lives? What degree of fruit is produced? We should strive to be the kind of disciples represented by the fourth kind of soil—the receptive soil that bears fruit.

In *Bearing Fruit*, I have identified seven places in the New Testament where the word *fruit* is found. The first chapter uncovers the cultivation process in John 15 by closely examining how believers abide in Christ. The remaining chapters explain each of the fruits: chapter 2, The Fruit of Repentance; chapter 3, The Fruit of Ministry; chapter 4, The Fruit of Sanctification; chapter 5, The Fruit of Righteousness; chapter 6, The Fruit of Good Works; chapter 7, The Fruit of the Spirit; and chapter 8, The Fruit of Praise.

Growing Up

Bearing Fruit is the third installment in the Growing Up series. Each book addresses different areas of spiritual development in a Christian's life. *Growing Up: How to Be a Disciple Who Makes Disciples*, the first book of the series, was released in November 2013. In *Growing Up*, I outlined the initial practices every believer should possess in making disciples who make disciples. *Growing Up* is divided into three basic sections. The first three chapters build a case for the necessity of making disciples. Chapter 4 deals with training yourself to become godly. The remaining six chapters, if incorporated into your life, will aid in developing a C.L.O.S.E.R. walk with Christ:

- *Communicate* with God through prayer
- *Learn* to understand and apply God's Word to your life
- *Obey* God's commands
- *Store* God's Word in your heart
- *Evangelize* (share Christ with others)
- *Renew* yourself spiritually every day

The C.L.O.S.E.R. acronym can be incorporated into any context, with any age group and maturity level. Every discipleship group (D-Group) begins reading *Growing Up* together. A chapter is discussed within the group each week. For resources, videos, and handouts to assist you in discipling others, visit: growing upchallenge.com.

Firmly Planted

Firmly Planted is saturated with theological insights, personal experiences, and practical applications to establish you as a stable, secure believer. Based on the conviction that a change of mind leads to a change of actions, the overall structure of the book is meant to ensure that readers are well-equipped to enter and thrive amidst any situation life deals them. The reader will be able to understand and apply biblical doctrines to everyday life. The book covers each of the following topics:

- Assurance of Salvation
- Three Marks of a True Believer
- Our Identity in Christ
- Overcoming Temptation
- Walking in the Spirit
- The External Enemy: The World
- The Infernal Enemy: The Devil
- The Internal Enemy: The Flesh

- Spiritual Warfare
- Praying in Spiritual Warfare

How to Use the Material

Ideally, the material in the book should be discussed within a D-Group: a gender-exclusive, closed group of three to six people who meet weekly. (For more information, see chapter 3 of *Growing Up* or visit replicate.org.) You can gather at someone's home, a restaurant, a break room at work, or at church for personal accountability, mutual edification, and spiritual enrichment.

As you study and grow, remember that you are not merely learning for your own benefit, but also for the benefit of others. Guiding others in their walk with Christ is a joy many overlook. The foremost way to make disciples is to become a disciple, and the only way to teach others effectively is to continue as a lifelong learner. We are closest to Christ when we are doing what he has commanded us to do, and the best way to learn is to teach.

The material in each chapter should be meditated upon and applied to your life. Don't just read for head knowledge. Ask God to help you understand what you're studying and apply it to your life.

If you do this, you'll bear much fruit—fruit that will last long after you're gone.

Chapter 1

HOW FRUIT GROWS
The Absolute Necessity of Abiding in Christ

A friend of mine builds effects pedals for electric guitar players. Using these pedals, with the click of a button or the turn of a knob, a guitarist can alter the sound coming from his instrument. He can cause it to chop like a helicopter, distort like a speaker turned up too loud, or echo like a sound resonating through an expansive cave.

The principle behind effects pedals is incredibly simple. Using what are called pickups, the sound from a guitar is turned into an electrical signal, then carried to an amplifier, which converts the electrical signal into an audible sound. The effects pedals sit between the pickup and the amplifier, altering the electrical signal that is eventually heard.

He told me about a time when he was building a pedal for a friend and, for some reason, it just wasn't working. He had connected all of the different capacitors, transistors, and resistors in the order they were presented on his schematic, secured the input and output jacks on the side of the pedal casing, and ensured that both the guitar and amplifier worked—but when he turned on the pedal to test it out, nothing happened.

He retested all of the connections, traced the path of the signal to make sure there weren't any problems in the wiring, and tested each element individually to ensure there were no faults in the circuit. Everything was perfect, except for one thing. He had forgotten to connect the power adapter to the wall. As soon as he did, the pedal sprang to life and functioned exactly as he'd designed it.

Sadly, many believers attempt to live the Christian life in a similar way: unplugged from the power of the Holy Spirit. One of the most overlooked aspects of the Christian life is the absolute necessity of abiding in Jesus in order to bear his fruit.

Abiding in Christ

In his Gospel, John records seven statements of Jesus in which he declared himself to be certain things. These are often referred to as the seven "I Am" statements:

- "I am the bread of life. No one who comes to me will ever be hungry, and no one who believes in me will ever be thirsty again" (6:35).
- "I am the light of the world. Anyone who follows me will never walk in the darkness but will have the light of life" (8:12).
- "Truly, I tell you, I am the gate for the sheep. . . . If anyone enters by me, he will be saved and will come in and go out and find pasture" (10:7, 9).
- "I am the good shepherd. The good shepherd lays down his life for the sheep" (10:11).
- "I am the resurrection and the life. The one who believes in me, even if he dies, will live" (11:25).

- "I am the way, and the truth, and the life. No one comes to the Father except through Me" (14:6).
- "I am the true vine, and my Father is the vinedresser" (15:1 ESV).

Notice what the seventh (and final) "I Am" statement says. Jesus calls himself a *vine*. The reasoning behind this will likely astound even the most seasoned believers. Let us explore it for a moment.

Christ as Our Source: The True Vine

Throughout the Old Testament, the nation of Israel was frequently likened to a vine. One of the most splendid examples of this is found in Isaiah 5, appropriately titled "The Song of the Vineyard." Isaiah begins the passage as the narrator, saying that he is singing about "my beloved" and his "vineyard on a very fertile hill" (v. 1 ESV). He describes the intentionality with which a vinedresser cultivates the finest crop: "He dug it and cleared it of stones, and planted it with choice vines" (v. 2 ESV). Anyone who has planted a garden understands both the care that goes into this process and the effort that is required. One does not accidentally grow a garden.

Beginning with verse 3, however, the speaker shifts from Isaiah to the Vinedresser (God). He states, "Judge between me and my vineyard" (ESV). The tone of the song likewise shifts. "And now I will tell you what I will do to my vineyard. I will remove its hedge, and it shall be devoured; I will break down its wall, and it shall be trampled down. I will make it a waste" (vv. 5–6 ESV).

Okay, but this is all poetry, right? It's just metaphor for thoughts and feelings and emotions, isn't it? No. Here is the kicker: the Lord proclaims, "For the vineyard of the LORD of hosts is the house of Israel, and the men of Judah are his pleasant planting" (v. 7 ESV). Isaiah then brings the passage out of the realm of metaphor and into the realm of historical fact, "Therefore my people go into exile" (v. 13 ESV). Look at what has happened. God planted his people, his vine. The vine started bearing bad fruit ("wild grapes," according to verse 4). No matter how many times Israel was brought back into God's graces, they always found ways to mess it up.

In John 15:1, Jesus's words, in light of this passage, have particular weight. Saying "I am the *true* vine" (emphasis mine) brings all of this discussion of Israel-as-vine into sharp relief. Where Israel proved herself unfaithful, Jesus proved himself to be her unblemished fulfillment as the true Israel. He is the perfect bridge between imperfect man and holy God.

Surely the disciples recognized this, right? Consider where they were moments before he spoke this: they were reclining at the Last Supper over *wine*. Luke 22 reveals that just before Judas went out to betray Jesus, he offered a physical analogy: "This cup is the new covenant in my blood, which is poured out for you" (v. 20). Jesus showed them that his very blood was the *new wine*, his very body the *true vine*. They had walked with him for almost three years and witnessed that every word he ever spoke came true, and now he was making a blatant reference to a well-established analogy. Surely they understood the symbolism.

Yet this would not be the first time they missed what was right in front of their eyes. After Jesus fed the five thousand and then the four thousand, for example, the following took place:

> They were discussing among themselves that they did not have any bread. Aware of this,

he said to them, "Why are you discussing the fact you have no bread? Don't you understand or comprehend? Do you have hardened hearts? *Do you have eyes and not see; do you have ears and not hear? And do you not remember?* When I broke the five loaves for the five thousand, how many baskets full of leftovers did you collect?" "Twelve," they told him. "When I broke the seven loaves for the four thousand, how many baskets full of pieces did you collect?" "Seven," they said. And he said to them, "Don't you understand yet?" (Mark 8:16–21, emphasis mine)

Historically, seeing and hearing the truth of God had not been enough to convince Jesus's disciples, but he was not about to let them miss it again. On the way to the garden of Gethsemane to pray for the final time before his death, Jesus taught one final, absolutely crucial lesson: he was the True Vine. But that was only part of the final truth he desired to communicate.

God as the Caretaker: The Gardener

"I am the true vine," Jesus said, "and my Father is the vinedresser" (John 15:1 ESV). The vinedresser—or gardener—has the job of caring for the vines and tending to the branches of his garden. Unless you are acquainted with grapes, however, much of the process may be a mystery to you, as it was to me. The *Old Farmer's Almanac* gives some insight as to just how arduous (and rewarding) the task of vinekeeping can be.

Planting Vines

First, one must construct a trellis. The *Almanac* states, "Grape vines will need to be trained to some sort of support to grow upward."[2] This structure and protection cuts the risk of obtaining diseases spread by ground-dwelling critters. The vines are to be planted six to ten feet apart so their roots and branches have room to spread; the hole should be twelve inches deep and twelve inches wide. The vinedresser is to periodically trim the top two or three buds while steadily watering the plants.

Second, for the first couple of years, the gardener's job is to keep the vines from producing fruit—that is, until the vines have been sufficiently established. For the first few years, the roots are not strong enough to support a fruit-bearing vine. They are to be pruned in March or April, before the buds swell and after the harsh winters. The *Almanac* continues, "Not only would vines run rampant without control, but canes will only produce fruit once."[3] Surprisingly, in order to ensure a high-quality product, as much as 90 percent of the previous season's growth should be pruned.

Here's the key: the more one prunes, the more grapes one will produce. In the first year, "cut back all buds except for 2 or 3. . . . Select a couple of strong canes and cut back the rest."[4] In the second year, you are to prune back all of the canes. "Leave a couple of buds on each of the arms. Remove flower clusters as they form."[5]

I think the point is clear. Planting a vineyard requires great care and attention, with special emphasis on frequent, dramatic pruning. So what do we learn from Jesus calling his Father the vinedresser?

Tending the Vines

After he has planted the vineyard, we see that God prunes his branches, which are his followers, in two ways. First, he cuts off the dead wood. If small branches grow among the living ones, diseases and insects can kill the plant. He breaks these dead branches off because he doesn't want anything to hinder the production of fruit. Consider the following biblical texts:

Do not despise the LORD's instruction, my son, and do not loathe his discipline; for the LORD disciplines the one he loves, just as a father disciplines the son in whom he delights. (Prov. 3:11–12)

Endure suffering as discipline: God is dealing with you as sons. For what son is there that a father does not discipline? But if you are without discipline—which all receive—then you are illegitimate children and not sons . . . No discipline seems enjoyable at the time, but painful. Later on, however, it yields the peaceful fruit of righteousness to those who have been trained by it. (Heb. 12:7–8, 11)

Second, he trims the living tissue. Some living branches can reduce the quality and quantity of fruit by robbing the vine of nutrients it requires to grow. As anyone who has endured suffering knows, this is painful. He severs off those *good* things from our lives so that we can enjoy the *best* things. How does God prune us, then, since we are not exactly sticks and leaves growing out of the ground? He removes the insects, bugs, diseases, and life-sucking sprigs from our life, which can be wasteful activities, ambivalent attitudes, and counterproductive habits. He eliminates anything that hinders us from bearing fruit to the fullest.

So often we find ourselves filling our schedules with busyness and frivolous activities. Perhaps it is something harmful, like substance abuse, compulsive shopping, pornography, or excessive drinking. Perhaps it's something less obvious, like selfish control in relationships or working long hours at the office at the neglect of spending time with family. Maybe he's pruning even more subtle things than those: laziness or a slothful attitude. Whatever the Gardener sees fit to prune, he will—for the sake of producing good fruit.

Believers: The Branches

By itself, a branch is weak and brittle. If it weren't for the fruit a branch may produce, it would be worth little more than a stick for whittling. You can't build a house or construct a bench with a branch. In fact, branches are only used for one of two purposes: bearing or burning. Either they are left on the vine to bear fruit or they are gathered into a bunch and burned.

What makes a branch useful is not what it is in itself, but how connected it is to the vine. You can see how Christ's analogy is taking shape, and Scripture affirms it repeatedly. We are the *bride* and Jesus is the *bridegroom* (Eph. 5:25–33), believers are the *members* and Christ is the *body* (1 Cor. 12), and we are the *sheep* and Jesus is the *shepherd* (John 10). By ourselves, we are nothing but kindling; connected to the vine, the body, or the shepherd, we find our purpose. Indeed, you, as a branch, can do nothing apart from him. The more quickly you realize this, the more quickly you will acknowledge your dependence on him and your need for his strength.

Fruit Inspection

So what is our role as a branch? In this metaphor, God's role is to plant and cultivate the vineyard; it is Christ who is the Vine, and we depend entirely on the Vine for strength. How does this happen? Jesus elaborates in John 15:4: "Remain in me, and I in you. Just as a branch is unable to produce fruit by itself unless

14

it remains on the vine, neither can you unless you remain in me."

The Greek word for "remain," as some translations put it, is a difficult one to translate into English. Of the 120 occurrences in the New Testament alone, the word is translated as *abide, remain, dwell, continue, tarry,* and *endure.* The word is used eleven times in the first eleven verses of John 15. Rather than trying to pin down an accurate English word for it, however, it would serve us well to figure out how it is we are to abide, remain, dwell, tarry, and continue.

When a person submits to the lordship of Christ, he begins to work *in* us so that he can work *through* us. When we make him our home, he takes up residence in us. Think of your home. Your home is your base of operation. It is a place of comfort, security, and familiarity. It is what you await after a long, difficult day. It is where you find refreshment and renewal. It is where you keep the things you love the most. If Christ tells us to *abide* in him, what he is saying is, "Draw all of your hope, security, satisfaction, joy, refreshment, and renewal from me!"

Just as we feel most protected in our homes, where we are comfortable and secure, we are strengthened likewise in Christ. But Jesus takes it a step further. He asserts that, not only do we find our comfort and security in him, but without him, we can produce nothing, and we prove that we're lost.

Fruitless Lives

Jesus offers a stern warning to those who think they can produce fruit apart from Christ's strength. He alludes to Ezekiel 15:1–8, in which God warns Israel (the incomplete vine) they will experience judgment if they don't produce fruit.

When Jesus says we can do nothing apart from him, he is not saying we can't do anything good in our own strength. There are millions of people around the world who do noteworthy things without Christ. What he is saying, however, is that on our own, we cannot manufacture fruit that God will accept. When you are separated from the vine, you are fruitless and useless to God.

Have you ever played the game Monopoly? It can be a lot of fun, but if you're like me, it can become a full-contact sport. At some point it can cease being an exercise in entertainment and become an effort to amass the most properties. It is about winning! Why? It's not just that we want to win; it's that we want our opponents to lose. If you play the game really well and you're savvy in property acquisition and hotel building, you win big—you may acquire every dollar of Monopoly money on the board.

However, were you to take all of that money to the grocery store to purchase your week's groceries, the cashier would not allow you to hand over that hard-earned Monopoly cash and leave with store-bought goods. You might respond, "You don't understand; I own hotels on Park Place and Boardwalk!" The store management would reply, "No, *you* don't understand! We only accept U.S. currency." The currency of the Monopoly world cannot measure up to the currency of the U.S. Mint.

Your self-righteousness is like Monopoly money in real life—it is acceptable currency in the game, but in God's economy it doesn't amount to anything. He requires a different set of currency. The currency in his kingdom is his righteousness. We can perform all the good deeds we desire in our own strength, but we will fall short of the "real currency" of heaven. Isaiah 64:6 asserts that "All of us have become like something unclean, and all our righteous acts are like a polluted garment; all of us wither like a leaf, and our iniquities carry us away like the wind."

Believers are expected to produce fruit. However, on our own strength, we are unable to produce fruit that is acceptable to God. A self-dependent branch is as useful to God as an unfruitful believer. Therefore, if there is no fruit in your life, it may be that you're an unbeliever to begin with. Repent of your sins, put your faith in Christ, and begin walking with him today!

Proving You're Lost

Jesus continues in John 15:6, "If anyone does not remain in me, he is thrown aside like a branch and he withers. They gather them, throw them into the fire, and they are burned." The Bible is filled with passages about the impending judgment for those who are unsaved. Here, Jesus reveals four of the areas of judgment reserved for those branches that bear bad fruit.

1. The branch is discarded; he is cut off from intimacy with God.
2. The branch withers; he dries up and has no joy or peace. He becomes lifeless and dead.
3. The branch is thrown into the fire. Fire has the unique property of destruction and purification. The makeup of the thing thrown into it determines which one will happen to him.
4. The branch is burned. Notice that Jesus doesn't say "burned up," as though the burning will cease when the branch is done burning. He merely says "burned," indicating an unquenchable, unceasing fire. He portrays a picture of punishment.

Some have tried to use this section of Jesus's teaching to say that a believer can lose his or her salvation—that through one's actions (or lack of them) the eternal security of one's soul can become jeopardized. In the second book of this series, *Firmly Planted,* I devoted the first two chapters to this crippling concept, but allow me to expand for a moment.

If this were a passage about the possibility of losing one's salvation, it would starkly contradict other passages like John 4:14, "But whoever drinks from the water that I will give him will never get thirsty again. In fact, the water I will give him will become a well of water springing up in him for eternal life"; John 10:28, "I give them eternal life, and they will never perish. No one will snatch them out of my hand"; and John 18:9, "I have not lost one of those you have given me."

Insisting that these words from Jesus imply that, once attained, salvation can be lost, not only disregards the other things Jesus said, but also the implications of the audience he was addressing. In the Upper Room he was not speaking to a mixed audience filled with both true believers and unbelievers. He wasn't speaking to his twelve disciples, for Judas had already gone to the religious leaders to turn him in. Jesus was speaking to eleven true believers. Additionally, he was not saying, "If anyone doesn't remain in me . . ." as a threat to strike fear in people. He didn't mean, "Once you come to me, you had better do everything to stay there, because otherwise I'll throw you out and burn you like chaff!" What he meant was, "If you don't remain in me, you were never planted in me to begin with."

Don't take assurance of our salvation as a license for laziness. In other places in Scripture, we are challenged to examine whether we are true or false believers. Ultimately, Jesus encourages us to examine our own lives to see if our fruit lines up with our lips.

John clarified this misunderstanding in 1 John 2:19, "They went out from us, but they did not belong to us; for if they had belonged to us, they would have remained with us. However, they went out so that it might be made clear that none of them belongs to us." Once you are firmly planted in Christ, no tempest will rip you away. It is not by the branch's strength that it remains attached to the vine, it is due to the health and strength of the *vine*. Once attached, you will always be connected, and will then be positioned to bear the fruit Christ would have you grow.

Producing Fruit

Thankfully, rather than being burned in a fire, we have another option. On our own strength, even the best we can offer is filth in God's eyes, for it is not bathed in his righteousness. However, should we rely on God's strength and trust in his promises, we suddenly find ourselves in a situation where we're producing fruit.

Jesus said in John 15:5, "The one who remains in me and I in him produces much fruit." In this verse, the point of Jesus's talk about vines and branches culminates. Look at verses 2, 4, 5, and 8—the good and the bad, the positive and the negative, the godly and the worldly are, in this context, determined by the fruit of one's life.

Bearing fruit is a sign of reproduction. Are you witnessing Christ's life in your life? If so, it will show on display. If a branch produces grapes, it's for others to eat or press into wine. We don't eat our own fruit; others do. Our fruit is for those around us. Our fruit is a sign of our relationship with Christ and is a tool for building up the people God has placed in our lives.

Every branch connected to the vine will produce fruit. The scope and degree of the fruit is dependent on the Lord, but every true believer will produce fruit of some kind.

Proving You're Saved

We need to address another common misconception about fruit: it implies a works-based salvation. According to this reasoning, if one's life is judged by the fruit he or she bears, then it must be the fruit that saves them. This is false and displays a misunderstanding of the text. It is not the bearing of fruit that saves a person. The fruit determines what vine the person is connected to. Are you rooted in the vine of Christ? Then you will bear good fruit. Are you bearing bad fruit? Then you may need to check your roots.

Jesus says in John 15:8, "My Father is glorified by this: that you produce much fruit and *prove to be* my disciples" (emphasis mine). I cannot press this enough: we do not go out and do good things to validate that we are believers. Rather, it is by the things we do as believers that they will know we belong to Christ.

Producing fruit—replicating Christ's life—is, as we have discovered, a work of God. It is up to the Gardener to water and fertilize the vine, to keep away hungry birds, to ensure the trellis that supports the plant is sturdy. In the same way, the fruit of our lives is not due to some impressive effort on our parts, but is ensured by the vine in which we have been planted.

The Nature of the Harvest

If we can say we have been rooted in Christ and we remain in him as he remains in us, then, according to John 15:7–8 we can, "ask whatever you want and it will be done for you. My Father is glorified by this: that you produce much fruit and prove to be my disciples." Remaining in Christ yields a life that is supernaturally fruitful in two ways: we see our prayers answered, and we bring immense glory to God.

Answered Prayer

My father loves to build and show classic cars. But when I was a kid, I wasn't interested in metal and rubber. I desired to talk with him about Legos, G.I. Joes, and model cars. Even though it was beneath him, he would stoop to my level to converse about things I loved. He listened when I talked about my plans for customizing a scooter, he played alongside when I set up mock battles with army men, and he participated in building Lego towers at the table with me. We regularly talked about Hot Wheels and constructed model cars together. He did this because he was my dad. He loved hearing about matters that were important to me.

Still, he longed for the day when we could discuss things that were important to him as well. Eventually, I matured and began to discuss topics he enjoyed. We worked together for many years, visiting car auctions, finding deals on vehicles, and customizing the bargains we would find. I wanted things that were dear to his heart and found that, in doing so, they became dear to my heart as well.

Our relationship with God is the same. Even though our conversation is beneath him at times, he listens to us. Still, he longs for the day when we will share his heart. In the 1993 film *Shadowlands*, the screen version of C. S. Lewis says, "I pray because I can't help myself. I pray because I'm helpless. I pray because the need flows out of me all the time, waking and sleeping. It doesn't change God, it changes me."[6] This is precisely how we understand prayer to work. We need to be sure that we're not twisting Jesus's words to imply that he is some spiritual genie waiting to answer all of our requests. Advocates of this perspective will say, "After all, he told us to ask for whatever we want and it will be done for us." It is also ammunition for those wishing to inspire disbelief: "Didn't your God tell you to ask for anything you want and it'll be done for you? Well, you asked for that illness to be cured and it wasn't, so he must not exist."

Remember the qualification that Jesus puts on this statement: we must *remain* in him as he *remains* in us. As we remain in Christ and he replaces our old heart of stone with a heart of flesh,[7] our heart becomes his heart. His desires become our desires. My friend David Platt put it this way: "Make your wants God's wants, and then ask for whatever you want."[8] When was the last time you listened for God's direction on a particular area of your ministry? So often we tell God *our* plans and discuss *our* wants instead of listening to his heart and making it ours. Abiding in Christ moves us from our own selfish desires to God's specific plan for us.

God Glorified

Since God owns the vineyard, plants the vines, tends the plants, and causes the fruit to grow, it follows that he gets the glory for it. No one picks a grape and says, "Wow, look at the coloring of that branch! I've never seen this shade of gray before. This branch really is spectacular." No one plucks an apple and says, "The shade of green on these leaves is breathtaking! Those are some sharp looking leaves." No one bites into a peach and says, "That peach did a great job growing. I've never tasted something so delicious!" Instead, they praise the one who cultivated the fruit.

The vinedresser is the most important person in the operation of growing grapes and is compensated well for his expertise, which takes years to nurture. Knowing what to cut and where to cut it is a skill that requires intense study and practice. Since God made you, he knows exactly what to prune and where to remove it from your life in order to make you grow. But hear this: whenever he applies those spiritual shears to your life, it hurts.

Pruning involves pain, but there is no other way to produce fruit. It is the most essential part of producing a good crop. David says in Psalm 119:67, "Before I was afflicted I went astray." He elaborates on this in verse 71: "It was good for me to be afflicted so that I could learn your statutes."

Sometimes pruning comes before we sin; other times, it comes after. Either way, it happens so that we can produce more fruit. Most Christians pray for God to bear much fruit through them, but few are willing to endure the pruning process. No one enjoys being under the knife. However, the results of pruning are for our benefit and his glory!

The point of John 15 is that pruning is for our good. In his book *John: That You May Believe*, R. Kent Hughes says,

> Supposing you eliminated suffering, what a dreadful place the world would be! I would almost rather eliminate happiness. The world would be the most ghastly place because everything that corrects the tendency of this unspeakable little creature, man, to feel over-important and over-pleased with himself would disappear. He's bad enough now, but he would be absolutely intolerable if he never suffered.[9]

The worst thing God could do to those he loves is leave them alone and allow them to continue as they are. He prunes us because he loves us.

What are the shears he uses to cut away the dross? The Word of God. The Word of God acts like a knife, according to Hebrews 4:12. After Peter delivered his

23

sermon to the men of Israel in Acts 2, the text records that "they were *pierced to the heart* and said to Peter and the rest of the apostles, 'Brothers, what should we do?'" (v. 37). The same instrument that calls lost sinners to the vine is the instrument that cuts sin from their lives. As disciples of Christ, we must set aside everything that diverts or distracts us from drawing strength from Christ. The reason God allows pain and suffering in our lives is to expose our need for him. He wants us to hold on to him, not anyone or anything else. *Before God can produce fruit in our lives, he must reveal dependence in our hearts.*

On Our Own Versus with Him

One day Jesus stopped at Mary and Martha's house—the same women whose brother, Lazarus, would be raised from the dead after being in the tomb for three days. Luke 10:38–41 tells us of this encounter:

> While they were traveling, he entered a village, and a woman named Martha welcomed him into her home. She had a sister named Mary, who also sat at the Lord's feet and was listening to what he said. But Martha was distracted by her many tasks, and she came up and asked, "Lord, don't you care that my sister has left me to serve alone? So tell her to give me a hand." The Lord answered her, "Martha, Martha, you are worried and upset about many things, but one thing is necessary. Mary has made the right choice, and it will not be taken away from her."

Notice the contrast in the text:

- Martha was serving; Mary was sitting
- Martha was worrying; Mary was worshipping
- Martha was hurrying; Mary was hearing

24

- Martha was busy with the work; Mary was attentive to the Word
- Martha was laboring; Mary was learning
- Martha was bothered; Mary was blessed

Maybe the reason you aren't bearing more fruit for God is because you have been spending too much time doing things on your own strength and not enough time abiding in his. Slow down and spend time with Jesus. Perhaps the church today is filled with Marthas, but is desperately in need of more Marys.

Chapter 2

THE FRUIT OF REPENTANCE
Preparing a Path for God

Billy Graham has been an example of a faithful preacher, father, and husband. He has avoided the scandals that have plagued so many televangelists, pulpit speakers, and religious leaders through the years. According to *TIME* magazine, he has preached to an estimated two million people in person, and an estimated two billion people via television, radio, or the Internet. During my seminary career, I studied Dr. Graham's preaching extensively. When I was accepted into the PhD program in preaching, I decided to write my dissertation on a critical examination of the evangelistic invitation, so naturally, his name came up.

I was overjoyed at the chance to go to North Carolina with Don and Rob Wilton to meet with Dr. Graham at his ranch. Spending about an hour and a half with him was a joy for me. At the end of our visit, Dr. Wilton looked at Rob and me and said, "I want you boys to pray for Dr. Graham."

It was humbling, to say the least. Whether or not you agree with a given president of the United States, you cannot deny the fact that this position demands an immense amount of respect. In October 2002, at Texas

Stadium in Dallas, Texas, Dr. Graham—at one of his final crusades—was introduced by President George W. Bush, at one point the most powerful man in the world. It was a compliment to the faithfulness of this man as an adviser to presidents through the years, but also to someone who has had an immense influence for the gospel.

I wonder who would introduce Jesus Christ if he were preaching at AT&T Stadium today? Would it be a president? A politician? A king or a queen? A rabbi? Of all the people God could have chosen to introduce his Son, he chose the most unlikely guy—John the Baptist.

John's introductory message would have been baffling to someone expecting to see the Savior of the world introduced like, well, the Savior of the world. Rather than preaching with fanfare, excitement, and bravado as he paved the way for the Messiah, John preached repentance. I want us to examine from Scripture what biblical repentance looks like.

A Voice in the Wilderness

In his Gospel, Matthew paints a great picture of the strange manner in which the coming Messiah was introduced. Let's take a closer look:

> In those days John the Baptist came, preaching in the wilderness of Judea and saying, *"Repent, because the kingdom of heaven has come near!"* For he is the one spoken of through the prophet Isaiah, who said: 'A voice of one crying out in the wilderness: Prepare the way for the Lord; make His paths straight!' Now John had a camel-hair garment with a leather belt around his waist, and his food was locusts and wild honey. Then people from Jerusalem, all Judea, and all the vicinity of the Jordan were going out to him, and

they were baptized by him in the Jordan River, *confessing* their sins. (Matt. 3:1–6, emphasis mine)

Before we discuss the italicized words, there are three characteristics we need to acknowledge about this bizarre man, two of which you may have noticed on your own.

First, notice that special attention was called to John's unusual appearance—both by our standards and by the standards of the day. I know you probably realize this, but camel's hair and brown belts do not go together. He would have gotten in trouble with the fashion police long ago. It's safe to say that John the Baptist wouldn't have worn a coat and tie to preach either, excluding him from preaching at some churches today.

Second, he had an unusual appetite: locusts and wild honey. Many suggest he would smother the locusts with local honey in order to sweeten up the crispy outer layer of the bugs. Some have tried to build a case that John wasn't actually eating little critters but the fruit of the so-called locust tree or a honey cake-type meal because of the similarities between the Greek word for locust (*akris*) and honey cake (*enkris*). Eating the flesh of the locust, however, was permitted under Levitical Law (Lev. 11:21), not to mention the poor in that region eat locust still today. It was obviously worth pointing out that in addition to dressing awkwardly and eating strange foods, he spoke with unusual authority, and that is evident in the text. His message was simple: *Repent!*

It is crucial to remember that based on his wardrobe selection and dietary preferences, John did not fit in with the upper class of Israel. We have no record of him being formally trained in the discipline of proclamation or scriptural exposition. He acquired no degree and possessed no political clout, yet he still made it a habit to boldly stand up to authority figures when they directly contradicted the Word of God (and that eventually led to his death, as seen in Matt. 14:1–12). John calling out the religious leaders of his day would be similar to a homeless man walking up to Billy Graham and telling him how to run his ministry. He was a wild man in the wilderness telling the religious elite they were out of line.

But notice the third characteristic about the strange man preaching in the desert. John's message is the exact same as that of Jesus when he began his ministry. Both men used the same imperatives to the crowd: *repent* and *confess*. Furthermore, they constantly spoke about the *kingdom of heaven*—which describes the rule and reign of God over one's life. John's message was not wordy, but brief. It wasn't calming but confrontational. It wasn't soothing, it demanded soul searching. He was not out to gain friends and gather followers, but to help people avoid eternal judgment for unconfessed, uncovered sin.

By better understanding the terms *repent* and *confess*, we will more fully comprehend the message of Jesus. And by understanding his message, we will root ourselves more deeply into his vine, so that we may bear the fruit of Christ at all times.

Repentance

Repent (*teshuvah* in the Hebrew and *metanoia* in the Greek) is the first command from both Jesus and John, and it refers to the pain and grief associated with an understanding and acknowledgment of someone's sin and the subsequent course correction. Literally, it refers to a change of mind that leads to a change of direction. It is an inward, deeply introspective understanding that produces an outward, measurable shift in your actions and desires.

Scripture displays countless pictures of repentance in action, but let's examine two that display the kind of action expected from repentance. In Acts 11:21, Luke explains that "the Lord's hand was with them, and a large number who believed *turned* to the Lord." Additionally, in 1 Thessalonians 1:9, Paul commends the church by telling them he has heard from everywhere "what kind of reception we had from you: how you *turned* to God from idols to serve the living and true God" (emphasis mine). *Turning* to the Lord exemplifies a course correction. It's an about-face.

Unfortunately, during medieval times, the translators of the Latin Bible decided to translate the word for *repentance* as "do penance." As a result, it influenced the church for years into thinking a person must do something in order to be forgiven.

This concept is entirely alien to the New Testament. The confession of sin is to be directed to God, and is more than merely speaking with your mouth. It is an entire change of direction. When you change the way you view sin and see it as God does—when you adopt the mind of Christ—you will alter the direction in which you are heading. In this way, thoughts and actions are intertwined. Sometimes you change your thoughts and your actions follow. Sometimes you change your actions and your thoughts follow. Regardless, repentance demands dramatic change.

Every person is already walking somewhere, so it isn't a matter of *getting started*; it's a matter of adjusting our direction. Perhaps you remember the movie *Speed,* starring Keanu Reeves and Sandra Bullock, that came out my senior year of high school. (I know I'm dating myself here.) In it, Sandra Bullock's character is driving a bus strapped with an explosive device that will detonate if the bus reduces its speed to let the people off. The passengers have to figure out how to move the people to safety, navigate streets, and avoid pedestrians while maintaining a speed of at least fifty miles per hour. Their only option is to change direction toward safer routes. Our lives are the same. You can't just *stop* walking down the path you're already on—you must change your direction and head toward safety.

We can't have it both ways in the Christian life— we will either walk in the way of sinners or walk in the Spirit. You can either continue on your current course or listen to the conviction that comes from God, repent, and correct your course toward him.

Do not be deceived, however, into thinking repentance is the work of man—something you do of your own will and on your own strength. That is not biblical, for repentance is the work of God in your life. In 2 Timothy 2:25, Paul says that God may perhaps grant people repentance. If God *grants* repentance, then it is something that originates with him, flows out of him through his Spirit, and empowers you to turn the wheel so that you can follow his path. In other words, God acts, and our repentance is merely a reaction to him.

An old Cajun preacher summarized repentance this way: "I'm sorry for my meanness, and I ain't going to do it no more." It's more than just turning, it's actually *moving* toward God, away from your sin. It's a change of lifestyle.

Confession

As we noticed in Matthew 3:5, people reacted to John's message of *repentance* by *confessing* their sins to God. Confession is not an event or action; it's merely the process of agreeing with God about our sin.

We confess it to him and acknowledge that we were wrong. Moreover, we express our desperate need for God's sanctifying grace in our lives. Confession is not a weekly habit, it's an hourly habit at times. The frequency with which a believer should confess his or her sins is the frequency with which sin occurs.

Dietrich Bonhoeffer, in his book *Life Together,* wrote that confession of sin is an essential component of discipleship. "He who is alone with his sin," Bonhoeffer says, "is utterly alone. . . . But it is the grace of the gospel, which is so hard for the pious to understand, that confronts us with the truth and says: You are a sinner, a great, desperate sinner; now come as the sinner you are, to the God who loves you."[10] The reason I argue for a gender-exclusive D-Group to be made up of three to five is to surround yourself with people who will speak candidly into your life by calling your attention to areas of failure, encouraging you to view your sin as God views it, and walking with you as you constantly adjust your course toward him.

John tells us how God responds to our confession: "If we confess our sins, he is faithful and righteous to forgive us our sins and to cleanse us from all unrighteousness" (1 John 1:9). When I surrendered my life to Christ, I thought I had to recall every single sin I had ever committed in the past. Can you imagine how terrible that would be? I'd have been there for all eternity just naming my shortcomings. How gracious is God, though, to base forgiveness not on our ability to remember, count, or name every transgression, but on the finished work of Christ at the cross!

The only reason we have access to a Holy God is because of the finished work of Christ on the Cross. When Jesus died for you, he died for the things you've done, the things you're doing, and the things you'll do tomorrow that fall short of God's standard. "You're forgiven," he says. "Now go and sin no more." Jesus is faithful and just to forgive you—no matter how big or small your sins are—and once you acknowledge the sufficiency of his forgiveness, your response will be to gratefully walk after him.

When I married Kandi, I recited, "I, Robby, take you, Kandi, to be my wife, to have and to hold from this day forward, for better or for worse, for richer, for poorer, in sickness and in health, to love and to cherish; from this day forward, until death do us part." What makes our marriage so gratifying is the trust and respect we have for one another. Are there times when I mess up? Absolutely. Does Kandi kick me out of the house because I promised to take out the trash and forgot to do it? No. Does she leave me for speaking to her in a disrespectful tone? No. I'm still her husband, but our relationship is negatively affected when I let her down. Until I confess my mistake, the relationship will not be mended.

Confessing sin to God is not a matter of perfectly maintaining our relationship but restoring the intimacy we once had with him. We bring ourselves back into close fellowship with him when we acknowledge our shortcomings and turn from them. Please do not believe the lie that we can add Christ to our lives without subtracting sin. That is impossible. In order to restore our constantly breaking intimacy, we must confess sin and repent of it. The longer we wait, the more we draw out the brokenness that comes from a damaged relationship. Proverbs 28:13 says, "The one who conceals his sins will not prosper, but whoever confesses and renounces them will find mercy."

Don't fool yourself. Until you admit that Internet pornography is a sin, you will be stuck with its debilitating effects in your life. Until you admit that lying is a sin, you'll suffer from the lack of trust of those around you, the stress of manufacturing fables, and the constant need to save face. Until you admit that drunkenness is a sin, you will never experience sobriety.

The way to know you have experienced true repentance, forgiveness of sins, and assurance that you are a follower of Jesus Christ is by pursuing an active, ongoing relationship with God.

The Evidence of Forgiveness

In Matthew 3:7–9, we see that one's relationship with God is the evidence of a changed life.

> When he saw many of the Pharisees and Sadducees coming to his baptism, he said to them, "Brood of vipers! Who warned you to flee from the coming wrath? Therefore produce fruit consistent with repentance. And don't presume to say to yourselves, 'We have Abraham as our father.' For I tell you that God is able to raise up children for Abraham from these stones!"

Once again, not mincing words, John explains two components of repentance: the affirmation of repentance, and what repentance prevents.

Affirmation of Repentance

There were two types of people who journeyed to see John the Baptist in the wilderness: sinners genuinely seeking forgiveness and the self-righteous seeking only to condemn. Two of the most prestigious groups in Jewish society—Pharisees and Sadducees—are present in this text. They are not interested in receiving from John information about how to be closer to God; they are there to question his message. Notice how the New International Version translates this passage: they were "coming to where he was baptizing" (Matt. 3:7 NIV), which stands in contrast to someone

35

who would come to him *for baptism*. John recognized this and called them out for it. "Repentance produces fruit," he shouted, "so show me your fruit! If you profess repentance, produce fruit consistent with that repentance!"

The fruit of repentance—good works, if you will—doesn't precede repentance but follows it. Once you truly repent of your sins and turn to Christ, you will begin bearing the fruit of the Spirit: love, joy, peace, patience, kindness, goodness, faithfulness, gentleness, and self-control (Gal. 5:22–23). You will be more generous in your giving. You will be quick to confess your sins and quick to forgive people who wrong you. You will be more expressive in your worship. You will be consistent in your time alone with God, nurturing your relationship with him. You will have a desire for holiness and purity, and you will be convicted when you fall short of it.

The religious leaders' refusal to repent proved that they were not dependent on God for their righteousness, but trusted in their own righteous acts. You can always determine the root of one's heart by the fruit of their life. In Matthew 7:15–20, Jesus warns of "false prophets who come to you in sheep's clothing but inwardly are ravaging wolves. You'll recognize them by their fruit." He asks a crucial, rhetorical question to illustrate this truth: "Are grapes gathered from thornbushes or figs from thistles? In the same way, every good tree produces good fruit, but a bad tree produces bad fruit." One can tell a tree by its fruit, a truth John uses to drive his point home: "A good tree can't produce bad fruit; neither can a bad tree produce good fruit." He concludes with a serious warning: "Every tree that doesn't produce good fruit is cut down and thrown into the fire." The word *fruit* is singular (we will study this in depth in a later chapter), even though it encompasses a multitude of things. You don't get to pick and choose the characteristics of God you display; you either display them or you don't. Your fruit is the sum total of your life.

Leon Morris, in his commentary on Matthew, posits, "John is not inviting people to pile up good works. He is looking for a change in the orientation of the whole of life that will result in fruitful living. John is making with some vigor the point that being present at a fashionable religious center is not enough. Lives must be changed. In view of the certainty of the wrath to come, people must forsake evil ways and live rightly before God."[11]

Bystanders by the bank that day were claiming allegiance to Abraham as a sign of their salvation. Some hold similar beliefs today by trusting in the assurance of living in a "Christian" country, being raised by a Christian family, and attending a Christian church. They may have even walked an aisle, signed a card, repeated a prayer, and been baptized years before. But without true repentance, walking an aisle is just exercising, signing a card is just practicing your autograph, repeating a prayer is just talking into thin air, and baptism is just getting wet. Without signs of repentance, all of these "Christian" actions are meaningless.

Make sure you are not determining your future by a prayer you prayed in the past. You see, even the most grievous sin you have ever committed is completely covered and forgiven by Christ the moment it is confessed to him and repented of (turned from), but the prayer of a nine-year-old means nothing if that person is not living for God today. Don't tell me what someone has done and expect it to be a measure of where their soul stands; measure it by their present life. True repentance will bear the fruit of repentance.

What Repentance Prevents

Matthew concludes this section by illustrating that repentance will prevent future eternal judgment. John says, "The ax is already at the root of the trees. Therefore, every tree that doesn't produce good fruit will be cut down and thrown into the fire" (Matt. 3:10).

Before chopping a tree down with an ax, you must lay the ax head next to the place you intend to chop. It allows you to properly stand in relation to the trunk so you can adjust your hands before striking. This happens the moment before chopping the tree down. The ax being poised, ready to strike at the root of the trees, is a picture of imminent judgment. The reason God will cut down a tree and throw the limbs into the fire is because a fruitless tree is a useless tree. In the same way, fruitless repentance is worthless repentance. Lip service means nothing to God if it isn't followed by fruit.

John the Baptist doesn't leave his audience without hope, however, for he concludes with a promise:

> I baptize you with water for repentance, but the one who is coming after me is more powerful than I. I am not worthy to remove his sandals. He himself will baptize you with the Holy Spirit and fire. His winnowing shovel is in his hand, and he will clear his threshing floor and gather his wheat into the barn. But the chaff he will burn with fire that never goes out. (Matt. 3:11–12)

John's baptizing was in preparation for the coming King. Baptism is an outward expression of an inward desire for change. John's baptism is not to get people wet; it is to show on the outside how they are changed on the inside. On the one hand, baptism doesn't save anyone, and on the other hand, failure to follow through with baptism doesn't prevent anyone from being saved. Believing in the gospel leads to salvation.

Weeping at the Threshing Floor

John makes an interesting point by mentioning the winnowing shovel and the threshing floor in this passage. In Israel, farmers constructed a threshing floor by digging a hole in the ground on a hill where the breeze would blow through. Pastor and author John MacArthur sheds light on this process:

> The soil would then be wetted and packed down until it was very hard. Around the perimeter of the floor, which was perhaps thirty or forty feet in diameter, rocks would be stacked to keep the grain in place. After the stalks of grain were placed onto the floor, an ox, or a team of oxen, would drag heavy pieces of wood around over the grain, separating the wheat kernels from the chaff, or straw. Then the farmer would take a winnowing fork and throw a pile of grain into the air. The wind would blow the chaff away, while the kernels, being heavier, would fall back to the floor. Eventually, nothing would be left but the good and useful wheat.[12]

The picture of a threshing floor helps us understand that when the Messiah comes, he will separate the wheat from the chaff, the goats from the sheep, the unbelievers from the believers. The unrighteous will go away to eternal punishment and the righteous to eternal life.[13]

For a Jew, John's reference to a threshing floor would likely have brought 2 Samuel 24 to mind, when David decided to count the men of Israel for military purposes—directly demonstrating his unbelief in God. Joab knew it was wrong and approached David to question him about the error of his ways. As a result, David was greatly convicted. "David's conscience troubled him after he had taken a census of the troops. He said to the LORD, 'I have sinned greatly in what I've done. Now, LORD, because I've been very foolish, please take away your servant's guilt'" (2 Sam. 24:10). Here, he acknowledges that he was in sin, confesses it, and asks God for forgiveness.

The parallel of this account is found in 1 Chronicles 21:

> Then the LORD instructed Gad, David's seer, "Go and say to David, 'This is what the LORD says: I am offering you three choices. Choose one of them for yourself, and I will do it to you.'"
>
> So Gad went to David and said to him, "This is what the LORD says: 'Take your choice: three years of famine, or three months of devastation by your foes with the sword of your enemy overtaking you, or three days of the sword of the Lord—a plague on the land, the angel of the Lord bringing destruction to the whole territory of Israel.' Now decide what answer I should take back to the one who sent me." (vv. 9–12)

This was the ultimate lose-lose situation and a reminder of the gravity of God's treatment of sin. Notice how David responds:

> David answered Gad, "I'm in anguish. Please, let me fall into the LORD's hands because his mercies are very great, but don't let me fall into human hands."
>
> So the LORD sent a plague on Israel, and seventy thousand Israelite men died. Then God sent an angel to Jerusalem to destroy it, but when the angel was about to destroy the city, the Lord

looked, relented concerning the destruction, and said to the angel who was destroying the people, "Enough, withdraw your hand now!" *The angel of the LORD was then standing at the threshing floor of Ornan the Jebusite.*

When David looked up and saw the angel of the LORD standing between earth and heaven, with his drawn sword in his hand stretched out over Jerusalem . . . (vv. 13–16, emphasis mine)

Can you picture this image in your mind? The angel sent by God for destruction is standing right there with his hand clutching a sword drawn high in the air, poised to strike. David looked up, was able to *see* this angel, and knew instantly it was his fault. He reacted appropriately:

David and the elders, clothed in sackcloth, fell facedown. David said to God, "Wasn't I the one who gave the order to count the people? I am the one who has sinned and acted very wickedly. But these sheep, what have they done? LORD my God, please let your hand be against me and against my father's family, but don't let the plague be against your people." (vv. 16–17)

David recognized his sin, wept over it, confessed it to the Lord, and repented of what he had done. John expected the same reaction from the Pharisees and Sadducees who came to the place where he was baptizing. And it is the only response that is appropriate once we realize just how desperately we need forgiveness.

Are you desperate for repentance like David was? Have you wandered from the intimacy with God that comes from a right relationship with him? You don't need to wait to be in a confessional booth or a church service; you can turn and confess your sin to him right this second. Repentance brings us into the presence of God, who promises, "Return to me, and I will return to you" (Mal. 3:7).

Chapter 3

THE FRUIT OF MINISTRY

A Ministry with No Regrets

The Seattle Times reported a story in November 2014 about Michael Leal, a student at Everett High School in Washington State who was suspended repeatedly for preaching the Bible, handing out gospel tracts—including a fifty-two-page pamphlet titled *How to Know God* in the lunchrooms—and for talking to fellow students about Jesus in the hallways between classes and at after-school events. A reporter stated, "The district's lawyers say his activities—including an amplified 20-minute extemporaneous sermon at a school 'car bash and bonfire'—have created a 'substantial disruption' at the school," the article says, quoting a letter written from the school to Leal's attorneys. He was suspended for two days. When he came back to school, the school said that he walked around at a volleyball game handing out "tracts to parents and students who wanted one."[14]

When his principal, Cathy Woods, confronted him after the volleyball game, she threatened that if he continued handing out tracts and religious materials, he would be breaking the law. Proselytizing students is frowned upon in Washington. "It has been well established by court precedent that students do not leave their free speech rights at the schoolhouse door," Leal's lawyers rebutted by stating his right to speak openly and freely about his religious convictions.

Leal engaged in other "expressive activities," according to the school, despite previous warnings, and was soon suspended for three days. Finally, on October 31, he was again caught handing out a tract to a student in math and was suspended a third time for "disruptive behavior."

Did you ever think you would see the day when kids would be suspended or expelled for handing out tracts at school? Leal's desire to proclaim God's Word was reported all over the world. News outlets across the country picked up the story and offered their commentary; some was negative, some positive, but the story spread, nonetheless.

Leal's story accurately illustrates the words of the apostle Paul in Romans 1. The faith of the Roman believers was being reported all over the world. Their courage to stand up for the gospel was noteworthy and a stark enough contrast to everyone else living in that location that people couldn't help but talk about what these Christ followers were up to.

I want you to be inspired to do the same as Michael Leal, the early Roman Christians, and many others who have gone before you, by not being ashamed of the gospel of Jesus Christ.

Ministry Heard 'Round the World

It may seem as though Paul, by using the word *first*, is setting us up for a long list of actions to perform. Soon, however, he abandons the order in his excitement to build up the believers he is writing to. Instead of filling a list or emphasizing certain points, he begins, "Before I get to the things I'm writing to you about, let me share my heart." His preface is unbelievably heartening to the believers who will soon be reading the letter.

> First, I thank my God through Jesus Christ for all of you because the news of your faith is being reported in all the world. God is my witness, whom I serve with my spirit in telling the good news about his Son—that I constantly mention you, always asking in my prayers that if it is somehow in God's will, I may now at last succeed in coming to you. For I want very much to see you, so that I may impart to you some spiritual gift to strengthen you, that is, to be mutually encouraged by each other's faith, both yours and mine. (Rom. 1:8–12)

The extent of the ministry of the Roman believers, according to this passage, stretched across the world. Of course, Paul probably did not literally mean "all the world"—he couldn't have known of the gospel's reach to the Tierra del Fuego in South America or the upper reaches of the Russian Arctic Circle. Paul was using hyperbole—an exaggeration for the purpose of stressing a point. By explaining to the Romans that their faith was being talked about all over the world, he was letting them know that people as far away as Asia Minor, where he was, were noticing how God was moving among them.

Paul then tells them of his desire to meet them face to face in order to impart a spiritual gift to them. Again, this is something we should not take out of context or misinterpret, as some have. He was not trying to meet up with them to give them a spiritual gift like speaking in tongues or prophecy, although many have translated this text to say just that. Paul envisions a more relational meaning.

The word for *gift* here is *charisma*, from which we get the word *charismatic*. It is frequently used to describe the gifts imparted by the Holy Spirit to the believer as discussed in 1 Corinthians 12 and Romans 12—miracles, tongues, prophecy, and healing—that are emphasized in charismatic churches. However, the word has a much broader meaning, as illustrated in 1 Peter 4:10: "Just as each one has received a gift, use it to serve others, as good stewards of the varied grace of God." God extends gifts to *each one* of us for the purpose of serving and building up others.

When we take the context into account, the true meaning of Paul's gift is discovered: his fellowship. Fellowship is the gift that Paul referred to when he wrote to the Romans, "For I want very much to see you, so that I may impart to you some spiritual gift to strengthen you, that is, to be mutually encouraged by each other's faith, both yours and mine" (Rom. 1:11–12). Encouragement from other believers was not just a nice option; it was absolutely necessary due to the constant persecution the believers were facing in the first century.

At the very least, this introduction is a reminder of our need for community and accountability that comes through fellowship with other believers. It also shapes how we do missions. Yes, it is important to financially support those in the field, but do not underestimate the role encouragement plays in the lives of the missionaries. When you visit, listen, pray, and lock arms with those serving in full-time ministry, you express how much you care about them. Everyone is not able to preach or sing, but everyone can listen and encourage those who are on the front lines. Thinking in this way motivates everyone to serve in some capacity.

However, we shouldn't stop with encouraging missionaries who are serving in a foreign country. When was the last time you encouraged the pastoral staff at your church? Normally the only time a church member speaks to a staff member is when there's a crisis or a concern in the church. As a pastor myself, I assure you that you will never know how much it encourages a staff member to receive a letter in the mail, an encouraging comment, a gift card, or a phone call.

Paul eventually made it to Rome, although perhaps not how he planned: in chains (see Acts 28). But as we see in other letters written from prison, Paul's infectious joy for the gospel of Christ is unhindered. He is overjoyed by the fruit of faithfulness the believers in Rome had been displaying, and is burdened for the lost people who lived there.

When Burdens Aren't Bad

As mentioned in his letter, Paul had attempted to visit the Roman believers on many occasions but was prevented. We are uncertain about what kept him from Rome, but we can conclude he genuinely desired to be with them.

Paul's motivation for traveling there was to "have a fruitful ministry among [them]" (Rom. 1:13). One translator paraphrases this text this way: "That I might have a harvest among you." In essence, he is saying, "I want to visit you to gather fruit!" Remember, fruit normally refers to Christlike character, as in the fruit of the Spirit, but in this context Paul expands the conversation of fruit to include conversions to the Christian faith from paganism or Judaism.

The fruit of Paul's ministry was *people*. He wasn't concerned with acclaim, riches, or great fame, but rather with seeing fellow men and women coming to a saving knowledge in Jesus Christ. Look at how he describes this in 2 Corinthians 3:1–3:

Are we beginning to commend ourselves again? Or do we need, like some, letters of recommendation to you or from you? You yourselves are our letter, written on our hearts, known and read by everyone. You show that you are Christ's letter, delivered by us, not written with ink but with the Spirit of the living God—not on tablets of stone but on tablets of human hearts.

There are only three things in this world that are eternal: God, his Word, and the souls of men and women. Paul understood the folly of investing in riches, for they can be taken away. He knew how wasteful it was to become wrapped up in worldly philosophy, for it was empty. Paul was making a lasting and eternal investment.

The Burden for People

Too often we translate the word *burden* or even *obligation*, as Paul said, as negative concepts. A burden is something heavy, something we are forced to carry. Paul, rather, does not view his burden as a weight or obligation. Instead his burden fills him with expectancy and joy!

In Romans 1:14, Paul draws two distinctions: Greeks versus barbarians, and wise versus foolish. Though *barbarian* has adopted a negative connotation because of its use as a descriptor for uncultured, brutish groups of people, Paul uses it to simply mean "non-Greek speakers." Paul contrasts those who do not speak Greek from those who do. Historically, Greek-speaking conquerors degraded those they had conquered and viewed them with contempt. However, Paul dissolves that distinction entirely. He maintains that he is equally obliged to the Greek speakers and the non-Greek speakers, just like every believer is as well.

He expands this equal obligation to both wise and foolish. Again, we understand that Paul is not putting anybody down here; he's simply drawing a connection between educated people and uneducated, or simple, people. Paul makes it plain that his obligation is not to one group of people but to all people, everywhere.

Do not apply this word *obligation* the wrong way. It would be easy to assume Paul is commenting, "I owe it to God to come talk to you, because I have received salvation from Him." This kind of thinking views salvation as a debt, when it is clearly anything but. Ephesians 2:8–9 says, "For you are saved by grace through faith, and this is not from yourselves; it is God's gift—not from works, so that no one can boast." Salvation is a gift—a *free* gift—which needs no repayment. Paul does not owe it to God to go talk to the Romans, but it would be missing the mark to say that he is not a *debtor*. The question is whom he is a debtor *to*.

Paul is not a debtor to God but to the Gentiles. If he were to cease being indebted to those around him, he would be disobedient to God's command to take the gospel to all people in all nations at all times.

General Booth, the founder of the Salvation Army, had the same passion Paul did. Queen Victoria once asked him what she could do for him. Imagine being in the presence of the queen and being an answer away from getting almost anything in the world. The rugged old man replied, "Your Majesty, some people's passion is money, and some people's passion is fame, but my passion has been men."[15] He was so intent on helping others that he didn't consider it a burden that he *had* to bear; rather, the great joy of his life was that he *got* to experience difficulty however often he was allowed to help those in need.

49

The Burden to Preach

Paul's burden went deeper than just reaching or interacting with lost people and believers alike. Specifically, he wanted to share Christ with them. He states in Romans 1:15, "So I am eager to preach the gospel to you also who are in Rome." In Paul's epistles there are two main instances in which he uses words that are translated as *eager*. One instance occurs in Acts 21:13, and means *prepared*. "Then Paul replied, 'What are you doing, weeping and breaking my heart? For I am ready not only to be bound but also to die in Jerusalem for the name of the Lord Jesus.'" The other use of *eager*—the one used here in Romans that is usually translated *ready*—means to have a keen expectancy to do something.

Paul was fully prepared to die, as seen in Acts 21, since he was sure he served faithfully and was confident at his death of being taken immediately into the arms of his Savior. On one hand, he couldn't wait to be called home to be with Jesus; on the other hand, he was probably not too *eager* to die, for he still had work to do, including ministering to the believers in Rome.

Paul did not view his work negatively. He was excited to preach the gospel with both his lips and his life. His eagerness was not that of a sightseer who anticipates the wonders he will behold, but the eagerness of a soul-winner receiving lost sinners from hell. He saw before him the plentiful bounty to whom he could preach and reap for the kingdom of God, and he couldn't wait to engage in that work.

Paul wasn't traveling on mission trips to check boxes, or add another thumbtack to his office map of places he'd traveled. He wasn't interested in boasting to friends back home or posting a humanitarian Facebook profile picture. He was going to share the gospel of Jesus Christ and advance his kingdom, and he was absolutely unashamed of the gospel he was sent to preach.

The Boldness of the Gospel

Paul demonstrates his conviction about the gospel in Romans 1:16–17, which states, "For I am not ashamed of the gospel, because it is the power of God for salvation to everyone who believes, first to the Jew, and also to the Greek. For in it the righteousness of God is revealed from faith to faith, just as it is written: 'The righteous will live by faith.'" He begins the verse with the word *for*, which is often used to justify a certain claim or offer a disclaimer before saying something particularly controversial (yet biblically sound). Why would Paul have to justify his message or offer a disclaimer to his readers? Some were questioning the message of the gospel because of how *simple* it was.

In 1 Corinthians 1:18, he reminded the church that "the word of the cross is foolishness to those who are perishing, but it is the power of God to us who are being saved." A few verses later, he continued, "For the Jews ask for signs and the Greeks seek wisdom, but we preach Christ crucified, a stumbling block to the Jews and foolishness to the Gentiles" (1 Cor. 1:22–23).

In 1 Corinthians 2:2 he states, "I decided to know nothing among you except Jesus Christ and him crucified." In *A Bible Commentary for English Readers,* we read this about that verse:

> Paul did not dwell on the miraculous in the life of Christ, which would have pandered to the Jewish longing for a "sign"; nor did he put forward elaborate "theories" of the gospel, which would have been a concession to the Greek's longing after "wisdom": but he preached a

personal Christ, and especially dwelt on the fact that He had been crucified.[16]

Paul was not ashamed of the gospel, nor was he ignorant to its power. In fact, he knew firsthand the power of the gospel was exactly in its simplicity—it didn't require fancy philosophy to explain it or fanciful miracles to confirm it. The resurrection of Christ was, and is, a reality that is self-sufficient and worth proclaiming. In the New Testament, to be ashamed was to be humiliated. It was also to heap undeserved shame upon oneself.

Shame

Humiliation can be deserved or undeserved. Deserved humiliation is the result of sin or poor choices we have made. If a husband commits adultery, when he returns to his wife and family to make amends, he will face humiliation—a reaction to the conviction that he has missed God's mark of holiness and purity. It is well-deserved, godly humiliation that leads to reconciliation through forgiveness.

Undeserved humiliation, on the other hand, is what we experience when someone shames us simply because they don't agree with what we believe. For Christians, many of us are rejected because of our belief in Christ. Some are shamed because of their proclamation of the gospel, something that an unbelieving world considers foolishness. But Paul reminds us that one day our humiliation in the world's eyes will be turned into vindication. Our faith in an invisible, personal, loving God will become sight, while every knee will bow and every tongue confesses that what we proclaimed—Jesus is Lord—is true forevermore.

Jesus used this word *shame* in Mark 8:38 when he said, "For whoever is ashamed of me and my words in this adulterous and sinful generation, the Son of Man will also be ashamed of him when he comes in the glory of his Father with the holy angels." If you have never been ashamed of the gospel, the probable reason, as D. Martyn Lloyd-Jones suggests, is not that you are "an exceptionally good Christian," but rather, that "your understanding of the Christian message has never been clear."[17]

It may be foolishness by the world's standards to put your complete faith and trust in a crucified man who rose from the dead, but that is where God's power resides. The gospel is not advice to pick oneself up by his or her own spiritual bootstraps. It's not a self-help system for recovery. It's not a feel-good message to experience your best life now. It is a message that promises your best life in the future. John MacArthur boldly states, "The only way we're living our best life now is if we are going to hell when we die."[18]

The word that Paul uses for *power* is the same word from which we get our word *dynamic*. The dynamic power of the gospel causes people who are dead to live. It gives hope to the hopeless and peace to the restless. Paul does not say that the gospel *brings* power, but that the gospel *is* power. When the gospel is preached, it is not simply words uttered about a man who died, but it is the actual power of God for salvation! It sets people free from the bonds of sin and death and brings us into the security of God's arms.

Remember the day you surrendered your life to Jesus? The cleansing power of the gospel erased the penalty of sin from your past and future alike. At that moment, the God of heaven inhabited your life with his Holy Spirit. On that day, Jesus took up residence in your heart. You had a collision with the God of the universe, and it left you permanently, inalterably, unashamedly *changed*. It left some identifiable marks in your life.

Let us say, hypothetically, that I showed up fifteen minutes late to preach a sermon, and I recounted the following story: "You will never believe what happened to make me fifteen minutes late. On the way to church today, I had a flat tire. As I was taking the spare tire out of the trunk, it bounced away from me, into oncoming traffic. I dodged two cars in an attempt to retrieve the tire, but the last one smacked me—and unfortunately for me, it was an eighteen-wheeler. I picked myself up from the cement several yards down the road, hobbled back to the car, changed the tire, and hurried to get here as fast as I could. Sorry I'm late."

The church would look at me and instantly recognize I was lying, because I bore no identifiable marks from the collision. I should have injuries, fractured limbs, and dislocated joints. I should be dead! If I bore no scars from the collision, the most likely conclusion is that the collision never happened at all.

If a person collides with the God of the universe at salvation, there will be visible marks on his or her life. When you come into contact with the One who spoke the world into existence, fixed the planets in place, counted the stars, breathes life into every living thing, parts the seas, shuts the mouths of lions, and rescues men from the burning flames of fire, there will be visible signs of that encounter. The gospel—the message that God came to the earth in human form, lived a sinless life, died on a cross, rose from the dead, and calls us to repent and believe—is that power. It leads to salvation "first to the Jew, and also to the Greek" (Rom. 1:16). God offers salvation to everyone who believes the message about him.

First to the Jew

Why is the message first for the Jews? When Paul says, "First to the Jew," he doesn't envision priority in salvation as much as he does order of salvation. Salvation came first to the Jews, then to the Gentiles. Both groups—the Jews and the Gentiles—are saved the same way: through faith in the Messiah, Jesus.

It is a misconception that Old Testament saints were saved through works—specifically, the works of the sacrificial system—and that after Jesus came, Gentiles were saved by faith. Salvation has always been the same. Old Testament saints looked forward to his coming and today we look back on his arrival. It is the same kind of faith. Even though Old Testament saints didn't know his name, the Promised One of God was the one in whom they placed their trust. Salvation is by faith alone; God hasn't changed the requirements to enter his Kingdom.

Hebrews 11:24–26 demonstrates an example of this: "By faith Moses, when he had grown up, refused to be called the son of Pharaoh's daughter and chose to suffer with the people of God rather than to enjoy the fleeting pleasure of sin. For he considered reproach for the sake of Christ to be greater wealth than the treasures of Egypt, since he was looking ahead to the reward." The difference between us and Moses is, as New Covenant believers, we look *back* on the Messiah named Jesus. The faith required to do so is the same as those who hadn't seen him yet.

How is This Gospel "Good News"?

In Romans 1:17, Paul states, "For in it the righteousness of God is revealed from faith to faith, just as it is written: 'The righteous will live by faith.'" Righteousness here is called God's righteousness because he is the source of it. Human righteousness is not enough—"a polluted garment," as Isaiah calls it (Isa. 64:6).

God's righteous standard renders the so-called good works of every human insufficient; no one can meet the standard of God's righteousness. Because Adam and Eve disobeyed God in the garden, the entire human race was plagued with sin and its effects. Paul tells us in Ephesians 2:1–2 that we were "dead in [our] trespasses and sins in which [we] previously lived." Similarly, Romans 3:10 and 23 states: "There is no one righteous, not even one" for "all have sinned and fall short of the glory of God." The problem is our heart, which is poisoned by sin and, as the prophet Jeremiah put it, "more deceitful than anything else, and incurable" (Jer. 17:9).

For this reason, God made a way for us to overcome the wickedness of the heart and depend on him to make us clean. He accomplished his plan by sending his Son Jesus as the perfect, spotless sacrifice for our sin. Jesus went in our stead to the death we deserved and conquered the eternal punishment that was coming our way. Those who acknowledge his sacrifice, repent from their sins, and place their faith in Jesus Christ will escape the wrath of God, alienation from the Father, hostility toward God, and separation from his Kingdom. They will be free from the bondage of slavery, impending danger, a wicked generation, a life of unrighteousness, and ultimately, *death*.

At the end of this section of Romans, Paul quotes Habakkuk 2:4 in reference to the manner in which the righteous will live. His message is clear: it is not by works, not by good deeds, not by "keeping on keeping on" that they will get by. It is by *faith* in the One who lived a perfect life. The fruit of their lives—righteousness—is not something they have accomplished; it is something they have been granted because of their faith in Jesus Christ!

Righteousness by Faith

The faith a believer has in the Messiah is not blind, as many critics like to call it. It is, instead, rooted in the facts of the Word of God. It is a faith that rests in Christ. Perhaps the reason some are ashamed of the gospel is because they don't understand the weight of that from which they have been saved.

Imagine vacationing on an Alaskan cruise ship with your spouse. One sunny summer day, you are on the deck enjoying the breeze, soaking in the sun, in awe of the scenery just off the bow of the boat. Suddenly, the ship collides with an iceberg. You are catapulted from the ship into the frigid waters, completely help-less since the safety of the ship's deck is multiple sto-ries above you. Your spouse yells frantically for help as you succumb to hypothermia and begin to sink into the deep waters.

Suddenly, a man in a wet suit dives off the top deck of the boat. He descends into the water and emerges a few seconds later on the surface, dragging you with him. He lifts you on board the ship by the rope attached to the life preserver and administers CPR on your breathless body, successfully resuscitating you to the cheers of everybody on board. Who gets credit for your survival? Is it you, who saved yourself by your sheer willpower and excellent swimming ability? Of course not. The honor goes to the one who jumped in after you. When the news media approaches you upon your arrival back home, you don't explain that you had it under control all along. That would be crazy! Rather, you would respond, "This man saved my life! I am alive because of him. I was on the doorstep of death, but he saved me!"

If you were interviewed on TV, you would shout from every platform you could find about the man who saved you. You would be unashamed to talk about it on any radio program. You would tell everyone who would listen about the man who saved your life.

Even more important than the lungs with which you breathe is the soul that will live on after they stop. If we'd be so quick to celebrate the one who saved our life, shouldn't we be even more excited to talk about the One who saved our souls? Live in gratitude for that gift. As a result, the shame people put on you for proclaiming the gospel will vanish as you focus your eyes on the One who selflessly, gloriously saved you.

one who

Chapter 4

THE FRUIT OF SANCTIFICATION
God's Work in Our Lives

It is remarkable what human beings have been able to accomplish over the years. Some of our feats are concrete: building remarkably tall buildings, constructing vehicles that can take us deep into the ocean, launching men and women into space. But some of the most remarkable accomplishments have been with animals—chimpanzees, in particular.

Washoe is one of the most famous chimpanzees of all time. Picked up by some soldiers in West Africa in 1966 and transported to the United States, she was adopted by a pair of doctors at the University of Oklahoma. While there, she underwent rigorous training overseen by professionals and soon, by the hard work of these remarkable human beings, Washoe became the first non-human to learn American Sign Language. She had learned around 350 signs by the time she died and was able to use them to communicate about objects like metal or a dog and actions such as running or crying.

Early in her training, Washoe's trainers were convinced she was merely mimicking what she had been taught. After several years, however, the staff at the University concluded that she was able to conceptualize—to produce and communicate her thoughts completely unprompted by her trainers pointing to an object. From the safety and comfort of her cage, where she had been given everything she needed to live—water, food, and companionship—Washoe signed her first three words of her own initiative: "Let me out!"[19]

It is natural for us to desire freedom. Nobody welcomes enslavement and imprisonment, especially to sin. Its cost is high—higher than anyone wants to pay—and it will always string you along further than you want to go. Thankfully, God made a way for us to escape. He designed us for freedom from sin, but not so we can roam about as we choose; rather, God designed us for freedom to serve him.

If we are designed for freedom, why do so many of the apostles call themselves "bond servants"? A bond servant is a person who is held in service to someone else without pay or any other kind of wages. This seems a bit like counter-freedom, doesn't it? Yet we see Paul, James, Peter, and Jude all refer to themselves with this term—and without shame. In Romans 6:15–23, Paul elaborates on this seemingly contradictory concept of freedom through slavery:

> What then? Should we sin because we are not under the law but under grace? Absolutely not! Don't you know that if you offer yourselves to someone as obedient slaves, you are slaves of that one you obey—either of sin leading to death or of obedience leading to righteousness? But thank God that, although you used to be slaves of sin, you obeyed from the heart that

pattern of teaching to which you were handed over, and having been set free from sin, you became enslaved to righteousness. I am using a human analogy because of the weakness of your flesh. For just as you offered the parts of yourselves as slaves to impurity, and to greater and greater lawlessness, so now offer them as slaves to righteousness, which results in sanctification. For when you were slaves of sin, you were free with regard to righteousness. So what fruit was produced then from the things you are now ashamed of? The outcome of those things is death. But now, since you have been set free from sin and have become enslaved to God, you have your fruit, which results in sanctification—and the outcome is eternal life! For the wages of sin is death, but the gift of God is eternal life in Christ Jesus our Lord.

Notice how Paul begins this section with a question: "Shall we sin now that we are under grace and not the law?" He is asking, "Okay, now that Christ has set us free, do we have license to sin whenever we want?" It is important to understand just what Paul means by the phrase, "under the law." To the Romans reading this letter from Paul, this was an unfamiliar phrase, not found anywhere in Jewish literature or traditions prior to its introduction in Romans, Galatians, and 1 Corinthians. It describes the relationship Gentile Christians have to the law.

Romans is a peculiar letter because it addresses churches that included both Jewish and Gentile believers. In the first century and before, Gentiles could become part of the Jewish community by being circumcised and taking on the yoke (or burden) of the entire Old Testament Law. Once they had committed in these two ways, they were called "God fearers." We see an example of a "God fearer" in Acts 10 in the person of Cornelius.

Think of the commitment required to become a God fearer: someone had to literally go under the knife—or the rock, as it may have been—and obey all 613 commandments spelled out by the Torah. These practices displayed that a person had sufficiently severed themselves from their past. These actions still did nothing to fix the sin problem. Instead, Paul shows us something else that does.

Slaves to a Master

When a slave was sold from one master to another, he was forced to abandon the decrees, commands, and desires of the previous one and fully adopt those of the one who purchased him. He became enslaved not only to the work of the new master, but also to his ideals and desires. This new master was not just the master of his activities, but of his thought processes too.

Since enslavement to one master requires complete commitment of both mind and body, it is impossible to have two masters—or even a 90-percent commitment to one and a 10-percent commitment to another. In our lives, there are two options for whom we can serve: we can either sell out completely to sin or, as Paul put it in this passage, to "obedience, leading to righteousness."

Paul makes it clear—we can't serve both sin and God. For the Christian who is saved under grace, obedience is not the means for salvation, but the measure of it. Our obedience doesn't perfect our salvation; our obedience proves our salvation.

Leon Morris said, "Paul's point here . . . is not so much that a slave had to obey his master, but rather that the master you obey shows whose slave you are."[20]

If sin is the pattern of your life, it demonstrates you are a slave of sin and are headed to a Christless place. If you obey God, you are a slave to him, as proven by the righteousness produced in your life.

Paul offers no wiggle room in this matter. He presents it as cut-and-dry; there is no straddling the fence between being a slave to sin and a slave to godly obedience. His words echo the words of Christ as recorded in the Gospels on several occasions: "No one can serve two masters, since either he will hate one and love the other, or he will be devoted to one and despise the other. You cannot serve both God and money" (Matt. 6:24). Elsewhere, he states, "Anyone who is not with me is against me" (Matt. 12:30). Jesus drew sharp distinctions on other occasions as well, asserting that we will either walk the broad road or the narrow one; we will either build our houses on sand or on rock; we will either produce good fruit or bad fruit. The wisdom behind this rigid distinction in Paul's letter to the Romans is common throughout Christian teaching, and is visible in other areas of life.

In the movie *Remember the Titans*, Denzel Washington plays the role of high school head football coach, Herman Boone. The movie, set in 1971, chronicles the forced integration of the previously all-white T. C. Williams High School in Alexandria, Virginia, and is one of the most memorable films of all time. In it, there is a scene in which a bus full of football players is about to leave for summer training camp. Suddenly, the arrogant, white, all-American Gerry Bertier started talking back to Boone and giving him flack. Boone finally stepped close to Gerry and asked him quietly, calmly, to his face, "Who's your daddy, Gerry?" Bertier whispered, finally, "You are."

In the scene, Boone was making the point that Bertier was about to experience a form of enslavement in his final year of high school football. It was no longer going to be the Gerry show, it was going to be about the team, and Gerry was just part of it. Every believer must also be able to answer the question, "Who's your daddy?" I have a pastor friend in Louisiana who would respond to people in the community calling him "brother" with, "Tell me who your Father is and I'll tell you if you're my brother." You only have one "daddy," according to Romans 6:16—sin or obedience. You are either a slave to sin, which results in death, or a slave to obedience, which leads to righteousness. There is no third option.

Escape from Sin

Paul reveals a profound insight into how we can escape the slavery of sin in Romans 6:17–18: "But thank God that, although you used to be slaves of sin, you obeyed from the heart that pattern of teaching to which you were handed over, and having been set free from sin, you became enslaved to righteousness." This is a remarkable passage, for the Roman believers were freed from the power of indwelling sin in their lives and now were able to obey the teachings of Christ. When Paul uses the phrase *from the heart*, he is illustrating what it looks like to completely give oneself over to something—the idea of putting complete faith in something. The day you became a follower of Christ, you submitted completely to the authority of the Word of God.

Paul uses the term *transferred to*, to describe a slave taken from the ownership of one master and put under the control of another, greater one. He strikes a balance between human responsibility and God's sovereign power. By the grace of God, you have been taken from under the yoke of slavery to sin, which is heavy and impossible to bear, and have been placed under the yoke of Jesus Christ, which is easy and light (Matt. 11:30).

In his letter to the Colossians, Paul uses many of these same themes to convey to believers what they have been liberated from, and what or whom they now have the privilege of serving. He puts this idea into a slightly different light, though:

> [May you be] strengthened with all power, according to his glorious might, so that you may have great endurance and patience, joyfully giving thanks to the Father, who has enabled you to share in the saints' inheritance in the light. He has rescued us from the domain of darkness and transferred us into the kingdom of the Son he loves. In him we have redemption, the forgiveness of sins. (Col. 1:11–14)

The fact that believers have been liberated indicates two things. First, you didn't liberate yourself; you needed somebody else to save your life. Second, you have been liberated from something to share in the inheritance of a greater kingdom.

A slave is unable to free himself. A person can't simply go to his master and request freedom, expecting him to take the request seriously. You couldn't barter or negotiate to convince the owner to set you free so you can follow someone else, even if that someone else is yourself. Likewise, when you are a slave to something, you are completely under its control.

In a village bazaar in India, a farmer brought a huge cage of quail to sell. Each of the birds had a string tied around its foot, with the other end of the string tied around a ring on an upright stick. The quail walked around in a circle, held captive by the string so they wouldn't fly away while being inspected by potential buyers. Nobody passing by showed any interest in them, though, until a Hindu Brahman came along. His compassion for the animals and religious respect for all life motivated him to inquire about purchasing all of the birds. After discovering the price, he said to the merchant, "I want to purchase them all." After paying the money, he instructed the merchant to set the birds free. Surprised, the merchant hesitantly bent down, cut the strings, and assumed the birds would fly away. But they didn't. The quail continued to march around and around in a circle, pecking at pebbles in the dirt. Finally, he had to shoo the birds off, but even then they only flew a few yards away and began marching in a circle again, just as they had done while tied to the stick.

When you ceased being a slave to sin and became, instead, a slave to Christ, you had to realize that you had been released from the shackles of sin by Christ. You are no longer enslaved in a cell but free to serve him. The day you surrendered your life to Christ, you submitted yourself to the lordship of Jesus. You were set free from the bonds of sin. It's for freedom that Christ has set you free!

Living in Freedom

It is easy to say, "Live like you are free," and leave it there. Yet Paul goes further. He tells the believer how they are to live after being set free from sin. The answer lies in offering our bodies to God for righteousness. In Romans 6:19 Paul continues, "I am using a human analogy because of the weakness of your flesh. For just as you offered the parts of yourselves as slaves to impurity, and to greater and greater lawlessness, so now offer them as slaves to righteousness, which results in sanctification."

Trying to grasp the process of salvation and sanctification in our finite minds is difficult. The very reality of an infinite God taking on human form to save us from the sinful nature that plagues us is *simple*, but it is not *easy*. When Paul says he is using a human analogy, he is not belittling the Roman Christians. He is doing everything he can to make such a divine concept plain to mortal minds. The *weakness of the flesh* is a natural limitation. Lack of understanding, in this case, is natural, for we are not built to understand everything as God does—but analogies help. And so Paul was more than happy to provide such an analogy, especially because he feared some of them were still enslaved.

Remember when you, at one time, offered yourself to moral impurity and greater and greater lawlessness? For some, it may have been more recent than others, and some may still be living in slavery to sin. Every person has experienced that burden, and the problem with offering your body to sin is there is no end to the negative repercussions.

The grip of sin on your life is evident in its nature. For instance, you cannot tell just one lie. At first it may be one, but soon you have to tell another to cover for it, and another after that. Sin has the devastating property of building on itself. Lust leads to envy, envy leads to covetousness, covetousness leads to stealing. Looking at porn is not a single occurrence; it is a downward spiral that starts with a picture, progresses to a site, culminates with a subscription, and ends with emptiness and broken relationships. Lay's Potato Chips was onto something when they said, "Betcha can't eat just one." Sin is just the opposite. It tells you, "Oh, you'll be fine. You can commit just one."

When I was at the height of my drug addiction, I had one overwhelming focus every day I got up that trumped every other desire I had. (My testimony can be found in chapter 1 of *Growing Up*.) The urge was greater than my desire to eat, hang with my friends, achieve success in the world, or meet someone I could spend my life with. I desired only one thing—to get high. My routine looked like this:

I would wake up around ten or eleven every day after a long night of drug use. I would call my supplier who lived in the projects in New Orleans, and attempt to score some drugs. On many occasions, he wouldn't have anything at the time because he was waiting for the shipment to come in, which would put me in a panic. See, the time from the last use of drugs to the onset of withdrawals is around twenty-four hours, which meant every day was a race against the clock. If I couldn't find drugs in that time frame, I would begin experiencing flu-like symptoms at first, which rapidly progressed to what is nothing less than hell on earth. I often tell people the pain that comes from drug withdrawal is not something the human body was meant to endure. It is self-inflicted torture, which I went to great lengths to avoid.

Before coming to Christ, you were a slave to money, lust, greed, power, pleasure, and fortune. But in the same way we gave ourselves as slaves to anything of this world, we must constantly, repeatedly give ourselves to God and righteousness. It is not a once-and-for-all decision; it is a daily one. An hourly one, even. You have to present yourself constantly to God, for your sanctification is a lifelong process.

I've heard it said that a funeral and coronation should be held every day of a believer's life; you must die to self and crown Christ Lord of your life. Paul speaks to this in Romans 12:1–2 when he writes, "Therefore, brothers and sisters, in view of the mercies of God, I urge you to present your bodies as a living sacrifice, holy and pleasing to God; this is your true worship. Do not be conformed to this age, but be transformed by the renewing of your mind, so that you may discern what is the good, pleasing, and perfect will of God."

The way we offer ourselves as slaves to righteousness is by seeking holiness, purity, and righteousness through the grace God provides. We abstain from anything that would hinder our relationship with Christ, for he only uses clean vessels. It is as Paul told Timothy, "Now in a large house there are not only gold and silver vessels, but also those of wood and clay; some for honorable use and some for dishonorable. So if anyone purifies himself from anything dishonorable, he will be a special instrument, set apart, useful to the Master, prepared for every good work" (2 Tim. 2:20–21). Are you living a clean life? Are you in right standing before God?

I want to hear God's voice and be led by his hand. I want to stand behind the pulpit from which I have been privileged to preach with all the power of heaven behind me. I avoid sinning not because I'm fearful of what God may do to me, but of what he may not do with me. I want to be used by him, and so I will do anything that will keep me eligible to be used by him. The benefits of living a life of holiness are out of this world, and there's no bad aftertaste. There's no lingering shame, no guilty conscience. You don't wake up apologetic and hung over or feigning for your next fix. Sin may satisfy for a season, but once its season is over, it descends into misery. Holiness, on the other hand, satisfies forever.

Even if you do not commit to holiness right this second, I implore you to do at least this: count the cost of sin before you engage in it. It could be the first step toward finding the only One who can free you from it.

The End Result

Paul continues, "So what fruit was produced then from the things you are now ashamed of? The outcome of those things is death. But now, since you have been set free from sin and have become enslaved to God, you have your fruit, which results in sanctification—and the outcome is eternal life!" (Rom. 6:21–22). Paul's question here could be rephrased in this way: What did you gain when sin was your master?

What do you gain from an adulterous relationship? A moment of pleasure, sure, but you also gain resentful kids, a devastated wife, a ruined reputation, and lifelong guilt.

What do you gain from Internet porn? You gain an instant of satisfaction and then instant self-loathing, an unrelenting need for more, and increasingly hardcore and frequent visuals.

What do you gain from alcohol or drugs? Sure, you gain a temporary release from pain, but then you throw up in the morning, nurse a hangover, fight withdrawals, and forget where you were and how you got to where you are.

What do you gain from lying? A moment of escape from the current situation, but a deepening hole that grows slick around the edges and the knowledge that only by swallowing your pride and admitting what you've done can you climb out. Yet each second spent digging is another step you will have to humble yourself.

Each of these paths will satisfy you for a moment, but they all lead you to the same end: death. Since sin is a master, as you serve it you earn a wage, and the wage earned for a life enslaved to sin is spiritual death. Eternal life, on the other hand, is not a wage at all—it is a gift from God. Eternal life is not something you earn, whether given the chance or not. Yet, every believer is still obligated to live a life of righteousness, for a life of righteousness is proof of one's salvation. You may not be there until you get to heaven, but if you are not moving toward holiness, you need to examine whether you are saved or not.

Martin Luther King Jr. liked to repeat this quote from an old preacher: "Lord, we ain't what we oughta be. We ain't what we wanna be. We ain't what we gonna be. But, thank God, we ain't what we was!"[21] King quoted this when talking about the Emancipation Proclamation, but what was true for the freedom of black slaves is also true for every person who is enslaved by sin. Whether you are one step into the journey toward holiness or twenty years into it doesn't matter; it's only by the grace of God that you are able to make the move in the first place. And once you are his child, you will remain his child forever.

Paul drove all of this home in one of the most-quoted salvation passages from the book of Romans and, perhaps, the whole New Testament: "For the wages of sin is death, but the gift of God is eternal life in Christ Jesus our Lord" (Rom. 6:23). Many use this verse in an evangelistic presentation like "The Romans Road." It does have a place in this kind of presentation, but its context is much greater. It is the crux of a larger passage that says grace does not give us license to sin. Rather, it frees us and enables us to pursue holiness and godliness. Sin always comes with a price tag; its wage is death. However, the alternative is something we cannot earn, but is given to us anyway: salvation and eternal life.

We are preparing to spend eternity with Christ, who gave himself so we wouldn't experience eternity without him. So why would we continue to sin? When Paul uses the word *wage*, it is similar to what describes the daily pay a soldier receives for his duty. It was a wage he earned by the sweat of his brow, by the soreness of his muscles, by the danger he repeatedly subjected himself to for the sake of his country. Imagine a cruel dictator with little concern for his men. He used them as a commodity for preserving the comforts of his own lifestyle and hurled as many of his men as he could at the enemy until they turned away. The wage for putting their lives on the front lines was death, because that is what most of them earned.

Sin pays the same wage for its slaves. The weekly paycheck for sin is separation from the fellowship of God, with the added perks of hurt, shame, destruction of your testimony, severed relationships, and a guilty conscience. The final payout for a life of sin is eternal separation from God in hell. On the other hand, according to this passage, a gift is something great, unexpected, and unearned that's given to the soldiers. On special occasions, such as their birthdays or anniversaries, an emperor would sometimes hand out a free gift of money to the army. It had not been earned; it was a demonstration of the kindness of the emperor.

If I were going to rephrase Paul's words to encompass everything we've exposed in this section, they would read like this: "If we were paid for what we earned, we'd get death; but out of God's grace, he has given us life." In order to receive the free gift of salvation, you have to realize the futility of striving on your own and simply accept it from God. The reward is freedom from sin and eternity with Christ.

As our discussion of sin comes to a close, allow me to quote two thinkers who have been influential in my thought on this topic. Warren Wiersbe wrote, "The answer to the problem of sin is not simply determination, discipline, reformation, legislation, or any other human endeavor. Victory comes through crucifixion and resurrection."[22] Charles Spurgeon recounted a parable of a king and one of his subjects:

A cruel king called one of his subjects into his presence and asked him his occupation. The man responded, "I'm a blacksmith." The king then ordered him to go and make a chain of a certain length. The man obeyed, returning after several months to show it to the monarch. Instead of receiving praise for what he had done, however, he was instructed to make the chain twice as long. When that assignment was completed, the blacksmith presented his work to the king, but again was commanded, "Go back and double its length!" This procedure was repeated several times. At last the wicked tyrant directed the man to be bound in the chains of his own making and cast into a fiery furnace.[23]

Sin will always take you further than you want to go, make you pay more than you want to pay, and cause you to stay longer than you want to stay. Like that cruel king Spurgeon described, sin demands a dreadful price: death. But the good news is that God offers you the free gift of eternal life through the death of Christ Jesus in place of the sins you should have had to pay for. If you are not a Christian, I ask you to consider the consequences of your sin. Then, perhaps, you will "believe in the Lord Jesus, and you will be saved" (Acts 16:31). This is a message worth sharing with others!

Chapter 5

THE FRUIT OF RIGHTEOUSNESS

You Only Grow in What You Know

A phrase that gets shared by pastors and church leaders is, "You must have a consistent prayer time." Sadly, it has become a cliché more than a practice. Think of men over the years who demonstrated extraordinary prayer lives. Elijah, the prophet, prayed and both turned off the faucets of rain and rained down fire from the sky. James, the half-brother of Jesus, was called "Camel Knees" because the flesh on his knees was calloused from the long hours he knelt in prayer. George Muller prayed in millions of dollars over a sixty-year span of ministry and spent every penny caring for orphans.

One person particularly worth mentioning is John Nelson Hyde. Many knew him as "Praying Hyde." He was also referred to as "the man who never sleeps," "the apostle of prayer," and perhaps every other title that could possibly refer to an intercessor. In a biography of John Hyde, Basil Miller wrote:

> Deep in India's Punjab region [Hyde] envisioned his Master, and face to face with the Eternal,

he learned lessons of prayer which to others were amazing. He walked on such anointed ground . . . for thirty days and nights in prayer, or ten days on end, or remaining on his knees for thirty-six hours without moving. When he returned to the field preaching from such seasons . . . he was thus possessed of a spiritual power which opened dark hearts of India to his message.[24]

If Hyde failed to see a person converted to Christ each day, he is said to have wept at night, begging God to save more.

If there were ever a man with an equal or more powerful prayer life than these, it was the apostle Paul. I frequently wonder what it would have been like to be in the room to hear this man bear his soul to God and surrender himself completely to his will. How fortunate for us, then, that we get a glimpse into Paul's prayer life as he explained the topic of prayer for those to whom he wrote.

What Burdened Paul's Heart

Before examining what Paul prayed for and how he went about doing it, it is worth examining what we *don't* see him pray for. There are no biblical examples of Paul praying for safety, security, or for cures to physical ailments. He never prayed for church growth, for more people in the pews of the churches he'd planted, for bigger buildings, or for more finances for his personal use. It is not that these things were unimportant to him—we have seen him speak of physical ailments, of being poor, of being in danger, and living in tumultuous times. However, for Paul, the key issue was *maturity*. He knew if he could get somebody to fall in love with Jesus and walk by the Spirit, all of the peripheral issues would fall into place.

The oft-quoted passage when Paul tells believers that all things will work together for the good of those who love Christ (Rom. 8:28) is him teaching this very thing: love Jesus with everything you have, give him all of your wants and desires, and leave the details to him. Even if it means you're going to die for your faith, you can trust it was for the advancement of God's kingdom.

He explicitly emphasized spiritual maturity to the church at Colossae, stating, "We proclaim him, warning and teaching everyone with all wisdom, so that we may present everyone mature in Christ. I labor for this, striving with his strength that works powerfully in me" (Col. 1:28–29).

The state of one's heart, as I have already discussed in previous chapters, will become obvious as you view that person's actions; so it is with maturity. A mature person lives for Christ, gives systematically to furthering God's kingdom, serves the church faithfully, and is not a consumer, but a contributor to what the body has to offer. Specifically, mature believers sing alongside their fellow worshippers, desire to grow through close fellowship with other people in a life group or a D-Group, and spend time in God's Word. Consider Paul's prayer for mature believers, found in Philippians 1:9–11:

And I pray this: that your love will keep on growing in knowledge and every kind of discernment, so that you may approve the things that are superior and may be pure and blameless in the day of Christ, filled with the fruit of righteousness that comes through Jesus Christ to the glory and praise of God.

What I want you to see in this chapter is that when you grow in the knowledge of God, your love for God deepens, and as a result, you live a life that pleases him.

The Foundation for Christian Maturity

At the beginning of that prayer in Philippians 1:9–11, Paul mentioned his wish for the believers to "keep on growing." This is a picture of *abundance*, like a river spilling over its banks or a cup overflowing.

It is *love* that Paul wants to see abound, because love is the crux, the climax of the Christian message. In fact, the God of Scripture, toward whom all believers strive to grow, not only loves but *is* love (1 John 4:8). Know also that love is not blind, no matter how many hit songs say otherwise. R. Kent Hughes speaks against this faulty thinking in *Philippians: The Fellowship of the Gospel*:

> Love of God is not the same thing as knowledge of God; love of God is immeasurably more important than knowledge of God; but if a man loves God knowing a little about Him, he should love God more from knowing more about Him: for every new thing known about God is a new reason for loving Him.[25]

If your father abandoned you at birth and you never got a chance to meet him—not even talk to him on the phone or exchange letters—you may have a longing to meet him, but you won't truly love him, since you do not know him.

The same is true of God. When I hear people say things like, "The man upstairs and I are tight," or, "If it wasn't for the Big Man in heaven . . ." I can't help but think, *Do you even* know *him? If you do, how can you talk about him so flippantly?* Because the Israelites knew God so well, they revered him so greatly that they couldn't even mention his name! Instead of calling him by his name, YHWH, they substituted "Adonai," which means "Lord."

The more you know God, the more you respect and fear him. Likewise, a person's knowledge of God determines their love for him. I am not speaking of a superficial love, but a love that is based on the Word and lived out through the Spirit. This is why an understanding of the Bible is so essential for spiritual growth— because it describes an untold number of aspects of God and gives us a way to hear directly from him. The one who loves him will want to know what he says, and will spend time *constantly* in the Word to understand him. Only then can we love him even more and want to know him even better.

Knowledge by itself, however, is not sufficient, for Paul mentions the word *discernment* right alongside it. Discernment, frequently referred to as wisdom or insight, plays an important role in distinguishing between what is right and what is wrong. Without wisdom, love is unable to rightly express itself to others.

Consider the following insight: all four of the letters Paul wrote from prison begin with a prayer for knowledge.

- "I never stop giving thanks for you as I remember you in my prayers. I pray that the God of our Lord Jesus Christ, the glorious Father, would give you the Spirit of wisdom and revelation in the knowledge of him" (Eph. 1:16–17).
- "For this reason also, since the day we heard this, we haven't stopped praying for you. We are asking that you may be filled with the knowledge of his will in all wisdom and

spiritual understanding, so that you may walk worthy of the Lord, fully pleasing to him: bearing fruit in every good work and growing in the knowledge of God" (Col. 1:9–10).

- "I pray that your participation in the faith may become effective through knowing every good thing that is in us for the glory of Christ" (Philem. 6).

- Philippians 1:9—"And I pray this: that your love will keep on growing in knowledge and every kind of discernment" (Phil. 1:9).

Notice the fullness of love and truth in each of these verses. You cannot say, "I don't get involved talking about doctrine or trying to understand God better—I just love Jesus." It's impossible to love somebody you don't know! You can't say, "I know Christ, but I don't know the Word." They are one and the same! The Word of God has been since the beginning (John 1:1), was made flesh and dwelt among us (John 1:14), and was greeted by John the Baptist by a lake in Judea with the words, "Here is the Lamb of God, who takes away the sin of the world!" (John 1:29). The more you know about God, the more you will grow to love him, and the more you will grow to be like his Son.

The Expression of Christian Maturity

On a basic level, discernment is the ability to decide between what is right and what is wrong. Present a person with a gun and ask whether it is worse to shoot a stranger or a pumpkin, and he'll likely answer that shooting strangers is unarguably worse. But as Paul mentions, discernment is given "so that you may approve the things that are *superior*" (Phil. 1:10, emphasis mine). Wanting the best for someone is often more elusive than determining what is right versus what is wrong, what is good in comparison to what is *best*.

When Solomon was presented with the problem of two women arguing over whose child they were holding, the good outcome would have been simply giving the child to the rightful mother, but using his God-given discernment (wisdom), he succeeded in also justifying which choice was right and making the other woman unable to continue her lie by suggesting the child be cut in two.[26] Paul wants believers to grow in knowledge and discernment from God to be able to demonstrate godly wisdom in their lives. He prayed that love would grow out of knowledge of God to inform their decisions on an hourly basis.

The word *approve* is used here to describe the process of testing gold by fire to determine its genuineness. It is like the word *examine*, which Jesus used in Luke 14:19 to describe the man who turned down an invitation to a banquet. "I have bought five yoke of oxen, and I'm going to *try them out*. I ask you to excuse me," he said (emphasis mine). Examination is not something that is a purely mental game but is something that is proven and demonstrated through action.

There are a lot of good things that you can do, but God helps you discern what is *best*, as Paul discovered. When he evaluated the good things in this life and compared them to his current relationship with Christ, he considered his past accomplishments to be rubbish.

> If anyone else thinks he has reason for confidence in the flesh, I have more: circumcised on the eighth day, of the people of Israel, of the tribe of Benjamin, a Hebrew of Hebrews; as to the law, a Pharisee; as to zeal, a persecutor of the church; as to righteousness under the law, blameless. But whatever gain I had, I counted

as loss for the sake of Christ. Indeed, I count everything as loss because of the surpassing worth of knowing Christ Jesus my Lord. For his sake I have suffered the loss of all things and count them as rubbish, in order that I may gain Christ. (Phil. 3:4–8 ESV)

This is an incredible picture of Paul's love for Christ that was increasingly greater than his love for the things of the world as his knowledge of Christ grew.

This kind of discernment plays out in our lives in many ways. Think of when you're dealing with someone who is battling an addiction. A loving mother and father may think that giving their addicted son money, paying his rent, and allowing him to live in their house with no strings attached are demonstrations of love, but they may actually quicken his death. These seem like good things to do for someone you love, for you want to provide for them and not see them struggle. But your very efforts to help might enable them to hurt themselves more.

Love, in this case, is what will be *best* for the person in question. It might not seem loving to cut them off and force them to either deal with their addiction or seek help, but it is. It will facilitate the means to make them better. Unfortunately, I see this entirely too often, and it is a picture of how desperately we need discernment to extend love toward others, to approve the things that are superior.

A Community of Christian Maturity

In order to have biblical community, there must be unity. In fact, the word *unity* is built into it! Unfortunately, it's something that is not given proper attention most of the time, especially when it comes to the important matter of purity and blamelessness.

Some might ask, "Doesn't being pure and blameless really pertain to people only on an individual, personal level?" When Paul calls for purity it is to be found in the church body at large.

Yet Paul isn't insinuating we can achieve sinless perfection; he is merely expecting the body of Christ to pursue purity and blamelessness. To be *pure* means to be "sincere without hidden motives or pretense,"[27] and communicates the idea of moral transparency. What does this mean in more concrete terms? There should be no envy in the body. There should be no rivalries or divisions in the body. We must treat one another with respect, and that sometimes means agreeing to disagree. We may not see eye to eye on worship music, clothing style for the pastor or church members, facial hair, sermon length, or carpet color, but we do not let any of these secondary disagreements hinder our unity in what matters: the mission of making disciples of all nations.

To be blameless means to be "without—and without causing—offense." It means we should strive to live upright lives. It governs both our own actions and our relationships with others whom we might cause to sin. It is dangerous to say we are responsible for the lives of all of our brothers, but we certainly are to behave in ways that will not intentionally cause offense to the people who interact with us, watch us, and otherwise scrutinize our lives. Being pure and blameless is not a self-help program or simply a self-improvement system. It is God's work in the church body.

God's Work in Christian Maturity

God may have ceased creation after six days, but he is certainly not out of reach for his creation; he is constantly working on us. If we imagine God as a builder, then we, those whom he created, are constantly under construction. Paul emphasized this point in Philippians 1:6 when he said, "I am sure of this, that he who started a good work in you will carry it on to completion until the day of Christ Jesus."

Listen to the hope contained in these words. No matter how good it is now, no matter how terrible, no matter how far away from improvement you may feel, the final chapter of your life is yet to be written. God is still working on you, and the best is yet to come—it will be finished on the day of Christ Jesus. Since God wants to do so much with us, we have to be sure we are allowing him to do his work in us. It is dangerous to settle for mediocrity.

According to folklore, Michelangelo entered his studio to examine the work of his pupils. As he came to the painting of Raphael, one of his aspiring students, he gazed at it longer than usual. Without warning, he took a paintbrush and stroked one word across the entire canvas: *"Amplius!"* which in Latin means "Larger!"[28] Michelangelo was not rejecting the work, for the painter contained great skill and the painting was good, but good was as far as it could go. The small size of the canvas had made the design on it appear cramped. It needed to be expanded.

The Lord may have to come to the canvas of your life and, on top of everything you think you've created that is good and worthy, paint *"Amplius!"* Your spiritual outlook may have become confined, and your vision of what God wants to do in and through you may be restricted by your lack of faith or limited spiritual growth. God wants to do more with you, so let him!

The Fruition of Christian Maturity

If we allow God to work in us, we prove we are planted firmly in his vine—and we will soon be bearing his fruit. Paul understood this, too, for he encouraged the church in Philippi to be "filled with the fruit of righteousness that comes through Jesus Christ to the glory and praise of God" (Phil. 1:11).

This phrase can be interpreted in two ways: righteousness is the *source* of our fruit, or righteousness is the *type* of fruit. Either righteousness precedes the fruit we produce or righteousness is among it. The text seems to support the second interpretation. The fruit produced from being planted in Christ is righteous behavior that is exemplified by God's people. It is a type of fruit, not unlike patience, kindness, gentleness, or self-control. Righteousness—stripped of all its heady theological overtones—is a right relationship with God, resulting in a right attitude toward others. Righteousness is demonstrating integrity in conduct and character.

Here's an interesting question: Why doesn't Paul say you *will* be filled with righteousness? Why does he say he *hopes* we are filled with "the fruit of righteousness"? It is an interesting question with a profound truth inside of it. The fruit is an expression of something inside; the fruit of righteousness is the result of God's righteousness at work in us.

When Paul looked at the church, he saw a beautiful grove of trees overflowing with fruit. He probably had in mind Psalm 1:3, which states, "He is like a tree planted beside flowing streams that bears its fruit in its season." He didn't see something that would just sprout temporarily and then be done; he saw a long duration of fruit production. A grove of trees does not pop up overnight, and a bountiful orchard isn't grown in a day. It takes years of tilling, sowing, watering, pruning, fertilizing, and caring to grow an orchard. Bearing the fruit of God is no different. It takes the cultivation of the Gardener to bear the fruit he desires.

Because the fruit is a result of the Gardener's work, it is not accurate to say the fruit the Philippian believers were bearing was a result of Paul's investment or even the working of individual believers. It was God's work, which is highlighted by Paul's use of the passive voice, that you will be "filled." The one filling isn't the one being filled—it has to come from outside. You cannot manufacture righteousness in your own life; only God can.

Whenever you browse the fruits and vegetables aisle, you can probably find a large list of chemicals and contaminants that has been sprayed on the produce at some point. The only way to ensure food is free from toxins is to look for an organic section. Organic produce is free from synthetic pesticides, bioengineered genes, petroleum-based ingredients, and sludge-based fertilizers. The presence of these things has been studied in recent years and has been linked to birth defects, nerve damage, cancer, and other illnesses that might occur over a long enough period of time.

This is the result of mixing something unnatural with the natural process of fruit production. In the same way, the fruit of righteousness is organic fruit grown by God. While the sanctification process is synergistic (us working alongside God), our labor and our fruit is, as Paul put it, "to the glory and praise of God." We are to praise God for working in us. The only work of man that God accepts is work initiated by him. The work that reaches heaven must be started there.

Good Work

Do not assume that because God accepts the work he initiates, there is no work left for you to do. I remember when I was younger, going to a lake to skip stones across the surface of the water. As the stone would skip, ripples would flow from each impact of the rock.

The choices we make are the same way. Every decision we make creates a ripple effect in our lives and the lives of those around us. The choices we make—and our actions—determine where we are and what we are becoming.

Habits are practices that will physically change your life. You may have heard the adage, "Work smarter; not harder." It has remained through time because of its truth, and it applies to spiritual growth as well. Even though it is God who grows us as Christians, we can plant ourselves in an environment for spiritual growth.

There are habits, and there are what Charles Duhigg calls "keystone habits."[29] Keystone habits set off a chain reaction of events that affect other areas of your life, like dominos stacked in a line on a table. Keystone habits are ones like working out, eating healthily, tracking calories, and making your bed after waking up.

So are there Christian keystone habits? Of course there are. Waking up early to read the Bible will help you see its ripples across your day. Memorizing Scripture will affect the reactions you have to different situations. Prayer is a habit that will affect your acquisition of wisdom, knowledge, discernment, and love for God and others.

The choices we make today—and make a habit to do every day—will change how we live tomorrow, and the next day, and the next. "Do a good deed of simple kindness," poet Joseph Norris said, "though its end you may not see; it may reach, like widening ripples, down a long eternity."[30] Make the superior choice today and watch it ripple, like the impact points of a rock flung across a lake, in your life and the lives of those around you tomorrow.

Chapter 6

THE FRUIT OF GOOD WORKS

Your Work Done God's Way for His Glory

For years Christians have been asking, "How should I pray, and what should I pray for?" Paul, as we have seen in his letters, offers us a helpful prayer guide. His prayers were to the point. He didn't beat around the bush when it came to speaking with God. He made a beeline to his purpose.

Billy Nicholson, the famous Irish evangelist, was in a large meeting where he called upon a man to pray who was noted for mentioning all the missionaries he knew in every one of his public prayers. "Brother so-and-so," said Billy, "will you please lead us in prayer, but keep it in the County of Donegal!"[31] Apparently, the man liked to catch up on his prayer life in the service.

Paul, in contrast, never seemed to rush when praying. Of course he was trying to save precious paper, but perhaps the reason behind his lack of "catch-up" praying was that he was constantly in an *attitude* of prayer. He told the church at Thessalonica to "pray without ceasing" (1 Thess. 5:17 ESV). It's as if his day began with "Dear Lord" and ended with "Amen."

In this chapter, we will see how he prays for God's will to be realized in their lives. Consider Paul's prayer in Colossians 1:9–13:

> For this reason also, since the day we heard this, we haven't stopped praying for you. We are asking that you may be filled with the knowledge of his will in all wisdom and spiritual understanding, so that you may walk worthy of the Lord, fully pleasing to him: bearing fruit in every good work and growing in the knowledge of God, being strengthened with all power, according to his glorious might, so that you may have great endurance and patience, joyfully giving thanks to the Father, who has enabled you to share in the saints' inheritance in the light. He has rescued us from the domain of darkness and transferred us into the kingdom of the Son he loves.

God's Will for All Believers

Right at the beginning of this passage, Paul demonstrates that praying is a privilege and an act of worship to God that displays our need for God and our inadequacy without him. Prayer is simply talking with God and making your requests known to him.

Paul says that he does not cease to pray for the people in Colossae. Think of your own prayer habits in relation to this. We are quick to pray during the difficult seasons in our lives, aren't we? When we're undergoing physical illness, pain and suffering, financial stress, moral failure, or division in the church, we tend to be like Paul: we pray without ceasing. However, when things turn around and start to go well, we are inclined to slack off in our prayer life. Paul encourages us, however, to pray continuously in the good seasons and the bad. We should never stop praying.

When Paul prays for these believers, he wants them to be "filled with the knowledge of [God's] will." When we hear the word *will*, we tend to think of our own future. Where we *will* live one day, what college we *will* attend, whom we *will* marry, what kind of job we *will* have, or where we *will* retire. It is not wrong to ponder these things in light of the gospel, but it can often foster a man-centered approach to our walk with Christ.

Most people discern the Lord's will for their lives like the old Scottish woman who went house to house across the countryside selling thread, buttons, and shoestrings. When she would come to a fork in the road she would toss a stick up in the air and go in the direction it pointed when it landed. One day, however, she was seen tossing the stick up several times. "Why do you toss the stick up so many times?" a passerby asked her. "Because," she replied, "it keeps pointing to the left, and I want to take the road to the right."

Too often we treat God like that. He is reduced to a utilitarian genie who is asked to grant every wish we ask for. So how can we know God's will? *We can read his Word.* His will for your life can be known by what he has already said to you. Paul gives us a clue to understanding the knowledge of God's will. It is found in "all wisdom and spiritual understanding."

The word *spiritual* modifies both *wisdom*, which is the capability to understand and catalog principles from Scripture, and *understanding*, which is the ability to apply those principles to one's daily life. Having knowledge is about more than simply confessing true beliefs. It is about putting what you know into action. In this way, having the knowledge of God is not about filling your mind with facts about the Word. It is knowing as much of the Word as you can so you can actively and intentionally live it out. "Having the knowledge of God's Word control our mind," according to John MacArthur, "is the key to righteous living. What controls your thoughts will control your behavior. Self-control is a result of mind control, which is dependent on knowledge."[32]

Notice what Paul said in Colossians 3:1–2 pertaining to this issue: "So if you have been raised with Christ, seek the things above, where Christ is, seated at the right hand of God. Set your minds on things above, not on earthly things." We need to understand where he was coming from when he wrote this.

When Knowledge is Misunderstood

In the first-century church at Colossae, there was an incoming challenge to the Christian faith called Gnosticism. Advocates of this philosophy were suggesting that in order to have the knowledge and wisdom of God, you must acquire *secret* knowledge that allowed you to transcend this materialistic world. The same thinking has crept into our churches today under the guise of New Age Christianity.

Paul attacks this at its root by saying that knowledge is not obtained by uncovering some hidden information or knowing a secret handshake. It is found in the Word of God! It cannot come about as the result of man's wisdom; it must come through understanding Scripture by the illumination of the Holy Spirit. There are sources of knowledge available to us at every turn. There are fields of academics devoted entirely to the study of knowledge, including fields wondering how we can know anything at all. Knowledge is celebrated on current events blogs and Wikipedia, on talk shows and in sports recaps. None of these sources are bad, but the Christian must find superior passion in the knowledge that comes from the Word of God.

It is easy to get caught up learning about God from every other book but the Bible. It is great to read biographies of great men of the faith, stories of amazing missionaries, essays of a theological nature, books written by pastors and apologists, and reports about the miraculous work of God around the world. But we mustn't pursue these things and neglect the truth of God's Word. I have been convicted about this myself—at times I have found myself caught up reading many books about biblical things while not reading the Bible itself.

In 2014, *Newsweek* magazine released an issue with a cover story by Kurt Eichenwald titled "The Bible: So Misunderstood It's a Sin." The article in *Newsweek* quoted renowned pollster George Gallup, saying, "Americans revere the Bible but, by and large, they don't read it."[33] This observation comes, amazingly, from a non-Christian publication! If even *Newsweek* can see it, should we not be grieved about this indictment of the modern American church?

Imagine what kinds of problems emerge from within a society that claims to love the Word but doesn't have any idea what it says, particularly what it says about God. Worse, I believe many Christians may know what the Bible says but refuse to take Scripture to heart. Just because we know *about* something and can even recite things from memory doesn't mean we will obey it. Warren Wiersbe warns against reading for the sake of filling the mind with information:

> In my pastoral ministry, I have met people who have become intoxicated with "studying the deeper truths of the Bible." Usually they have been given a book or introduced to some teacher's tapes. Before long, they get so smart they become dumb! The "deeper truths"

they discover only detour them from practical Christian living. Instead of getting burning hearts of devotion to Christ, they get big heads and start creating problems in their homes and churches.[34]

Friends, we need to be careful that we are not so heavenly minded that we are no earthly good, as the old saying goes. Many don't need another Bible study guide to teach them theological truth; you need to invest the Bible you've studied into the lives of others around us. It is for this very reason that discipleship is essential for spiritual growth. It is a peculiar fact that we learn best by teaching something, perhaps because it forces us to really understand a concept before handing it off to someone else. You grow by investing what you know into the life of those around you. If you want to know the will of God for your life, know the Word of God first and obey it. What follows will certainly alter, permanently, the course of your life.

The Effects of a Surrendered Life

Remember what Paul says in Colossians 1:10: "So that you may walk worthy of the Lord, fully pleasing to him: bearing fruit in every good work and growing in the knowledge of God." Having a thorough knowledge of the Word of God, even having it hidden in your heart, will cause some peculiar things to happen: you will discover that you will begin thinking and acting differently. You will handle conflict and hardship with a level of grace you never thought you could display.

When the Word of God gets into you, it changes you: it produces fruit others are able to see. Your understanding of Scripture is not shown by how well you can quote verses or engage in theological discussion—it is displayed through your walk with God.

Bearing Fruit

Something we've seen repeatedly so far is that God produces fruit through us when we plant ourselves in an environment for growth. It's not a matter of achievement with our own hands and through our own strength. What's important is what you allow God to produce *in* you. Ministry is something that is received, not something that is achieved; it is a gift to us, not our gift to God.

Jesus would agree with that statement. He says in John 15:4–5, "Remain in me, and I in you. Just as a branch is unable to produce fruit by itself unless it remains on the vine, neither can you unless you remain in me. I am the vine; you are the branches. The one who remains in me and I in him produces much fruit, because you can do nothing without me."

Paul echoes this sentiment in two passages. First, in Ephesians 2:8–10 he states, "For you are saved by grace through faith, and this is not from yourselves; it is God's gift—not from works, so that no one can boast. For we are his workmanship, created in Christ Jesus for good works, which God prepared ahead of time for us to do." Second, Paul states in Philippians 2:12–13, "Therefore, my dear friends, just as you have always obeyed, so now, not only in my presence but even more in my absence, work out your own salvation with fear and trembling. For it is God who is working in you both to will and to work according to his good purpose."

It is God who works in *you*! You do not walk in your power, and you do not produce ministry by your own hands. Martin Luther asks and answers poignant questions with clarity in regards to this sometimes difficult issue in the lyrics to his hymn, "A Mighty Fortress Is Our God":

Did we in our own strength confide
Our striving would be losing,
Were not the right Man on our side,
The Man of God's own choosing.
Dost ask who that may be?
Christ Jesus, it is He.
Lord Sabaoth His name,
From age to age the same.
And He must win the battle.[35]

Faithfulness to God leads to fruitfulness, which is handy since he is the one who plants us, sustains us, waters us, prunes us, and shines on us. None of the fruit you produce is produced on your own, for you cannot produce any fruit. God alone can produce fruit in you. So be faithful in the vineyard or ministry in which you are planted, for God brings the harvest.

Growing in Knowledge

In years past, the church gauged someone's spiritual maturity by how many services or Bible studies they attended. Churches selected deacons based on how "faithful" they were to attend. However, as we have unfortunately discovered, frequent church attendance does not always amount to spiritual maturity.

If you read a novel and fail to understand the individual words without any context, you can't rightly say you understood the book. You must grasp what the author is trying to say, the subplot of the characters, and what makes the plot move forward, to say the least. In the same way, learning or hearing biblical information doesn't produce spiritual growth. Exponential spiritual growth doesn't happen through the introduction of new information or Bible facts, but through repetition and reiteration of deep spiritual truths.

Many churches across the world every single weekend have created a problem among the people who attend their services. I call it Bloated Christian Syndrome. Although people should be biblical scholars because of all the information they're fed each Sunday, sadly, they emerge having learned almost nothing. Let's see how Bloated Christian Syndrome works.

Let's pretend that you are heading to an average American church this Sunday morning. You hear some music, followed by a forty-or-so-minute message about a given topic, and then head to Sunday school, where you hear another lesson from the Sunday school curriculum. Since you are one of the "faithful," you return that evening after lunch and your Sunday nap to hear the pastor's next topic through the book you've been studying on Sunday nights. On Wednesday night you come back to church to have a prayer meeting and hear a devotional one of the members prepared during the week or took from a devotional book, and then you wake up early on Thursday to attend a coffee shop Bible study group you've joined that is on an entirely different topic. This is all in addition to your daily Bible reading, Scripture memory, and discipleship group books since, as we've said, you're one of the faithful.

Are you beginning to see the problem? By the time you get around to Sunday again, you won't even be able to tell the points from the sermon, let alone remember all of the biblical truths you've been exposed to that week! We have bought into the lie that we grow by the digestion of new information alone. But growth requires much more than that.

Jewish rabbis taught in a much different way: they believed that rehearsing older lessons was just as important as—if not more important than—learning new ones. One rabbi is quoted as saying, "He who reviews his lessons a hundred times is not like him who reviews his lessons a hundred and one times."[36] Professor Shmuel Safrai supports this rabbinical method of information transformation, which is known by the fancy word *pedagogy*:

> Individual and group study of the Bible, repetition of the passages, etc., were often done by chanting them aloud. There is the frequent expression "the chirping of children," which was heard by people passing close by a synagogue as the children were reciting a verse. Adults too, in individual and in group study, often read aloud; for it was frequently advised not to learn in a whisper, but aloud. This was the only way to overcome the danger of forgetting.[37]

Without notebooks to record, computers with which to type, or iPads to read, first-century students in a Jewish school relied on repetition and recitation for understanding. It was common for students to have, by the time of their thirteenth birthday, most of (if not all of) the Torah committed entirely to memory. This incredible capacity for memorization was made possible by constant repetition.

The Jewish Talmud, which is a commentary on Old Testament Scriptures, cites the importance of reviewing information frequently: "He who studies the Torah and does not review is like one who plants and does not harvest."[38] It is for this reason I recommend sermon-based life groups so strongly.

A church pays someone who has been trained in the craft of constructing a Spirit-led message and delivering it to the people. He spends fifteen to twenty hours a week doing nothing but that: researching, studying, praying, citing, wordsmithing, and checking every aspect of the message for scriptural accuracy and godliness. You come on Sunday morning to hear that message delivered by the pastor. We cannot run the risk of diluting the message that the Spirit has delivered to the people by scurrying off to lunch early or by getting another lesson laid on top of it in small groups/Sunday school. In a sermon-based small group, the curriculum is prepared as a complement to the message delivered from the pulpit, and thus the repetition begins.

In his book *Amusing Ourselves to Death*, Neil Postman argues "that television has habituated its watchers to a low information-action ratio, that people are accustomed to 'learning' good ideas [even from sermons] and then doing nothing about them."[39] This is illustrative of one of the problems with modern Christianity. It is not the gap between what we know and what we don't know, for we know an awful lot about a lot of different things. The more concerning gap is the one between what we *know* and what we *do*. We have, perhaps, become indoctrinated beyond our obedience.

Here is the model for biblical growth: The more you know him, the more you love him. The more you love him, the more you obey him. The more you obey him, the more he manifests himself to you. You start with only as much information as you currently have—you put as much faith as you have in as much of Jesus as you know, and he will take it from there, so long as you let him.

Patient Endurance

Returning to Colossians 1:11–12, Paul writes, "Being strengthened with all power, according to his glorious might, so that you may have great endurance and patience, joyfully giving thanks to the Father, who has enabled you to share in the saints' inheritance in the light." Since we've been examining how Paul prays, let's take note of the fact that he doesn't pray for the believers to be removed from trials and tribulations, but rather for them to have the strength to endure them. There is only one way to endure a trial with a glad heart—not by fixating on the trial itself, but by focusing on what it will produce in you: patience, steadfastness, and a reliance on God's strength.

Steadfastness is a word that applies specifically to how we deal with problems. Here are a couple of pertinent questions to see how you fare in the area of steadfastness: Are you patient with the problems that arise in your life, or do they frustrate you? When you have to wait on something to happen, do you do it with glad expectation or with impatience? When God's power comes into your life it gives you the power to wait, to trust him with your problems and frustrations. His timing is perfect and his patience is infinite. He can handle it, I assure you.

Endurance, however, applies to how we deal with people. With the onset of God's power in your life, He will enable you to endure without grumbling those things that people so often cause us to grumble about. It is the kind of patience a wife demonstrates when her husband forgets a task he's promised will get done, the kind of patience a parent has with a child when he fails to meet a household expectation. If you have endurance in dealing with others, you will not yield to outbursts of anger toward people who hinder or hurt you. It characterizes an attitude that does not retaliate in spite of injuries or insults.

The Serenity Prayer, popular in addiction circles, says, "God grant me the serenity to accept the things I cannot change, courage to change the things I can, and wisdom to know the difference." The Serenity Prayer highlights the key aspects of steadfastness and endurance: bearing patiently with situations that are out of your control, changing them when you can, and relying on God's wisdom to differentiate between the two. Do you want to practice endurance? Drive in your car on the interstate during rush hour and time yourself to see how long it takes before you get frustrated or mad at another driver.

Malcolm Forbes once said, "Diamonds are nothing more than chunks of coal that stuck to their jobs."[40] By this he means that coal, when subjected to enough heat and pressure over a long enough period of time, becomes a diamond. Not that we like to compare ourselves to a lump of coal, but don't we all want to become like diamonds, patiently enduring pressures and hardships so God can turn us into something precious for his use?

Since we've examined steadfastness and endurance in depth, let us reinsert these words into the context of prayer. Most of our prayer requests, it seems, are for God to remove suffering and pain—perhaps for us, perhaps for someone we know. However, notice that Paul never prays that way. He understands that God's divine instrument for molding believers into the image of Christ is suffering. Paul points out in Romans 5:3–4 (ESV) that "suffering produces endurance, and endurance produces character, and character produces hope" . For this reason, James 1:2 tells us to "consider it a great joy" when we encounter suffering. What a different mentality than we have when we ask God to alleviate pain and suffering!

More prominent than pain and suffering, however, is the struggle in the church that comes from discontentment. We are perpetually busy, always looking for something bigger and better, faster and stronger. We're incessantly in a rush to go nowhere. It may seem like a problem of the modern age, but as mentioned in chapter 1, Martha struggled with this very thing in Luke 10:38–42. In this passage, Martha was busy preparing the meal, managing the party, and putting out the place settings for the guests that included none other than the Savior of the world. In the middle of her work, she glanced over at Mary, who was simply sitting at his feet. Her mind instantly jumped to the fact that this woman was being lazy and sitting around when there was work to be done. She said to Jesus in verse 40, "'Lord, don't you care that my sister has left me to serve alone? So tell her to give me a hand.'" The Lord answered her, 'Martha, Martha, you are worried and upset about many things, but one thing is necessary. Mary has made the right choice, and it will not be taken away from her'" (Luke 10:41–42). Be patient, Jesus tells her. It is okay to sit and be patient; to be still and know that I am God.

Joyful Gratitude

The final point in this section of Paul's letter is about being grateful—giving thanks to the Lord. He says we are to be grateful that we are qualified to share in the inheritance of the saints in the light. The word *qualified* here is in the present tense, which indicates that this is something we share now. If you are qualified for something, you are made sufficient for it or authorized to share in it.

It is a big deal that in Christ we are qualified to share in this light, because we weren't always. At one point we were unauthorized to share in the inheritance of the saints because we were "dead in your trespasses and sins in which you previously lived according to the ways of this world, according to the ruler of the power of the air, the spirit now working in the disobedient. We too all previously lived among them in our fleshly desires, carrying out the inclinations of our flesh and thoughts, and we were by nature children under wrath as the others were also" (Eph. 2:1–3).

But the story doesn't end here, when all hope seems lost and we are doomed to face God's wrath. Paul continues, "But God, who is rich in mercy, because of his great love that he had for us, made us alive with Christ even though we were dead in trespasses. You are saved by grace! He also raised us up with him and seated us with him in the heavens in Christ Jesus, so that in the coming ages he might display the immeasurable riches of his grace through his kindness to us in Christ Jesus" (Eph. 2:4–7).

Prior to Christ, we were alienated from the inheritance. But after his death, burial, and resurrection we were granted access to God through Jesus. By repenting of our sins and putting our faith in Christ, we were adopted into the family of God, despite our unworthiness on our own.

For this reason alone, thankfulness should define every believer. We should be marked by an attitude of gratitude for the weight of the great inheritance that comes our way freely, and we should be quick to give it away out of our great thankfulness. G. K. Chesterton once remarked, "When it comes to life, the critical thing is whether you take things for granted or take them with gratitude."[41]

Chapter 7

THE FRUIT OF THE SPIRIT
The Flavor of the Fruit

Preachers are pretty good at asking rhetorical questions—questions that aren't meant to be answered directly, but rather internalized for the purpose of making a point. Rhetorical questions have been used for thousands of years by people of various professions to drive home a thought or concept in an audience.

Think of this question in the context of a preacher's sermon, at the end when he's concluding: "Who is the Holy Spirit to you?" There might be soft music playing, an attitude of reverence, and quiet reflection in the air. Some people are probably checking their watches to see what time they'll get out. Others are praying, internalizing the question, asking the Holy Spirit to be real in their lives, and so on.

Now, consider the question under different circumstances, when it was asked a bit more pointedly, and with the expectation of an answer. Walter Lewis Wilson was a doctor in the beginning of the twentieth century who was agonizing over his fruitless efforts at witnessing for Christ. One day in 1913, a French missionary was visiting in his home and asked the question posed above to him: "Who is the Holy Spirit to you?" Wilson gathered that it probably wasn't a rhetorical question, judging by the way the missionary expected an answer. So he replied, "He's one of the Persons of the Godhead . . . the teacher, guide, and third person of the Trinity." A textbook answer.

But his answer wasn't what the missionary was looking for. "No, you haven't answered my question," this missionary responded. "Who is the Holy Spirit to *you?*" Wilson responded the only way he knew how: with honesty. "He is nothing to me. I have no contact with Him and could get along quite well without Him."

At the beginning of the next year, on January 14, 1914, Wilson attended a message given by James M. Gray, a pastor and the future president of Moody Bible Institute. He was preaching from Romans 12:1. Gray stated, "Have you noticed that this verse does not tell us to whom we should give our bodies? It is not the Lord Jesus; He has His own body. It is not the Father; He remains on His throne. Another has come to earth without a body. God gives you the indescribable honor of presenting your bodies to the Holy Spirit, to be His dwelling place on earth."[42]

Wilson returned to his house and lay prostrate on the carpet. There in the late hours of night, he said, "My Lord, I have treated You like a servant. When I wanted You I called for You. Now I give You this body from my head to my feet. I give you my hands, my limbs, my eyes and lips, my brain. You may send this body to Africa, or lay it on a bed with cancer. It is Your body from this moment on."[43]

Two ladies came to Wilson's office the next morning selling their advertising services. He promptly led both of the ladies to Christ, an event that served as the beginning of an extraordinary life of evangelistic fruitfulness. He later founded Central Bible Church in Kansas City, Flagstaff Indian Mission, and Calvary

Bible College, along with writing a best-selling book. He wrote in his journal, "When I surrendered my life to the leading of the Holy Spirit on January 14, 1914, it was much greater than the change that took place when I was saved on December 21, 1896."[44] Think of the implications of this story for a moment and then consider the following:

- Isn't it amazing how many Christians, especially in the United States, attempt to accomplish God's work without the Holy Spirit?
- Isn't it amazing how much you and I attempt to do without the assistance of the Holy Spirit?

It is essential to walk in the Spirit to produce God's fruit. But don't take my word for it. Let's examine what the apostle Paul said, instead.

The Battle That Rages in the Believer

There is a battle going on in the heart of every believer. It is the battle between the flesh and the Spirit of God. Consider Paul's words in Galatians 5:16–17:

> I say then, walk by the Spirit and you will certainly not carry out the desire of the flesh. For the flesh desires what is against the Spirit, and the Spirit desires what is against the flesh; these are opposed to each other, so that you don't do what you want.

There are two kinds of fruit people bear: the fruit of a lost person and the fruit of a saved person. The way you determine the root of one's heart is by seeing the fruit of one's life. Jesus reminded us that we will know a tree by the fruit it bears.

So what does Paul mean when he talks about "flesh," then? He provides a list in Galatians 5:19–21: "... sexual immorality, moral impurity, promiscuity, idolatry, sorcery, hatreds, strife, jealousy, outbursts of anger, selfish ambitions, dissensions, factions, envy, drunkenness, carousing, and anything similar." He continues by saying that "those who practice such things will not inherit the kingdom of God."

Paul's final words in that section have been used by many attempting to support the idea that a believer can lose his or her salvation.[45] This argument is disarmed, however, by the Greek word *prasso,* translated here as "to do." In the Greek, this word speaks of a repeated or continuous action. Hence, *doing* refers to the pattern of one's life—the whole of a person's actions—rather than a single, isolated act. It is the continued, habitual, remorseless practice of sin that identifies a person as having never genuinely repented and been saved. I cannot emphasize this enough: you do not work for salvation, you work *from* salvation! But the fruit we bear is an indicator of the condition of our hearts.

A Subtle Tactic

When Paul instructs us to walk by the Spirit and not by the flesh, he's talking about the sanctifying work God does by removing those desires as we yield to him, and by which he molds us into the image of the Son. The more he sets us apart, the more fruit we bear.

The more fruit we bear, however, the more fruit the enemy will be looking to steal to use for his own devices. But remember that stealing isn't always obvious. Not all robbery is a bank heist. Sometimes stealing is subtle.

I heard about four teenagers who snuck into a produce farm late at night and spread out across the field. One young man picked up a ripe watermelon and handed it to his friend, who was waiting in the darkness, who passed it to the next guy, who passed it to the next guy, who deposited it into the trunk of the car idling on the side of the road. Even if the farmer had been watching the field at that moment, he wouldn't have been able to see their delicate and silent operation. Before any time had passed, they had a dozen huge watermelons and drove off into the night.

Fruit-stealing happens more often than we realize—not only with real fruit, but with what the Bible calls spiritual fruit. Satan doesn't want the fruit God grows to be on display in our lives. As soon as we begin to develop these spiritual virtues, the devil uses his tactics to steal them away from us by tempting us to sin. The fruit of the flesh are the deeds of the flesh. They are as evident as the fruit hanging off a tree, and they cannot exist on the same tree that is bearing the fruit of God.

The Blessings of Walking in the Spirit

Let's consider how Paul says a believer can avoid producing the fruit of the flesh. The language he uses in the Greek is authoritative and forceful. It is as if he is saying, "Take this to the bank. I'm putting my stamp upon it." When you walk by the Spirit, he says, there is no chance you will *ever* fulfill what the flesh desires (Gal. 5:16). The reasoning behind this assertion is simple. The fruit of the Spirit and the fruit of the flesh cannot occupy the same space: you will either walk by the Spirit or you will walk by the flesh. Paul wants us to realize the enormous blessings of walking by the Spirit.

After listing fifteen deeds of the flesh, Paul contrasts them with the graces of a Spirit-filled life, starting in Galatians 5:22–23: "But the fruit of the Spirit is love, joy, peace, patience, kindness, goodness, faithfulness, gentleness, and self-control. The law is not against such things." Paul does not recommend working harder at producing good fruit or fighting against producing the fruit of the flesh. He actually suggests that the believer should stop working in their own strength altogether. You can't do anything on your own. Your good works are filthy rags to the Lord. Instead of working with all your might against the desire of the flesh, you need to yield to the Spirit of God. Tim LaFleur, my disciplemaking pastor, frequently says, "The Christian life is either easy or impossible. It's impossible if you're doing it in your own strength, but it becomes easier as you allow God to work in you and through you."

Nine virtues are listed here, but notice the number of *fruit* Paul introduces. Does he say "the *fruits* of the spirit *are*," or does he say, "the *fruit* of the spirit *is*"? Both words are singular in the passage: the *fruit* (singular) and *is* (singular). It signifies that all of these virtues are unified and are within the believer. Every born-again Christian has the potential to produce fruit that manifests in multiple ways.

The Fruit of the Spirit

The first three fruits mentioned—love, joy, and peace—are habits of the mind. The second three—patience, kindness, and goodness—are virtuous deeds expressed to others. The final three—faithfulness, gentleness, and self-control—describe the general conduct of the believer. Let's look at each of these briefly.

Love

Love is a virtue that actually covers all of the characteristics that follow, much like the greatest commandment covers all of the law God laid down for His people. If you have love, if you *truly* have love, the rest of the fruit will come about naturally. It is interesting to think Paul could have simply left this list at "love," and moved on.

Love is the most-used word in Paul's vocabulary. Throughout his letters, he used it as a noun seventy-five times and as a verb thirty-four times. As believers, we should possess love for our fellow believers because God first loved us unconditionally. We are to take the immense love we've been shown and extend it to other people. When we lack love, it is a disgrace to the Lord Jesus, who is the epitome of love.

Joy

Paul regularly used the word *joy*. One glance through Philippians and you'll notice that he used it repeatedly. From prison, he wrote, "Rejoice in the Lord always. I will say it again: Rejoice!" (Phil. 4:4). Joy is not circumstantial; it is a state of mind. Paul was saying, "I can be in prison or a palace, and I can still be joyful." The word *joy* in Greek is the word *charis,* the same place we get the root word for *grace.* Those who have experienced the grace of God know that our only response to it is joy!

Peace

The Hebrew word for peace, *shalom,* is quite different than the English word. *Shalom* is actually another word for wholeness. In the Hebrew sense, peace does not imply the absence of wars, persecution, or violence, just like being peaceful doesn't mean there is no pain. True peace comes for the Christian from a right relationship with God that will extend to a right relationship with others. If your vertical relationship is right with God, your horizontal relationships will follow.

Paul elsewhere connects our justification (remember that word from our discussion a few pages back?) with peace from God. Romans 5:1 reads, "Therefore, since we have been declared righteous by faith, we have peace with God through our Lord Jesus Christ."

These three words—*love, joy,* and *peace*—form the bedrock of the Christian life. Our way of life is built from them: Love is the foundation, joy is the superstructure, and peace is the crown of all.

Patience

Patience, in my opinion, is the greatest outward indicator of one's sanctification. It is the ability to deal with cantankerous and difficult people, to be long-suffering with people who don't deserve it, to be loving toward those who are rebellious, and to not take offense at inconsiderate actions or words.

This indicator of our sanctification demonstrates the internalization of the grace we've been shown. Nothing about us deserves the long-suffering patience God has shown us, but we've received it anyway. Showing patience to others is a marker of our gratefulness for this immense gift.

Kindness

Kindness goes hand in hand with long-suffering. It is the idea of being mild and meek in our disposition towards other people. It is extending humble respect to others regardless of their ethnicity, color, creed, or economic status. The key ingredient in kindness is *humility*—not thinking of yourself as superior to those around you.

Jesus was the model of kindness. Think of how many times he was asked, "Why are you hanging out with *those* people?" Think of how many times he has demonstrated mercy and kindness to *you*.

Goodness

The word *goodness* is found four times in the entire New Testament, with Paul being the author of each of them. We extend goodness to someone by going the extra mile for them. If kindness is the attitude with which we should treat others, goodness is the method. We should be kind in our relations with those around us, and we should treat them well.

Faithfulness

The root of faithfulness is the word *faith*—being loyal to and trusting in God. This fruit is especially important to me because, as a full-time minister of the gospel of Christ, my faithfulness to God must trump my fear of man. It is as important to stand strong in my calling in the famine as it is in the harvest. The greatest gift a pastor can give to his church is not his preaching ability, his pastoral grace, his counseling knowledge, or his ability to lead member meetings. His greatest gift to the church is his personal faithfulness to God.

After he had been serving in India for eight years, William Carey wrote a note to his friend saying, "Pray for us that we may be able to be faithful to the end."[46] He was seeking to attain the status of Paul, who wrote, "I have fought the good fight, I have finished the race, I have kept the faith."[47] True faithfulness will position you at the end of your life to declare the same thing Paul did.

Gentleness

Gentleness is another word for meekness—not in action or behavior, but in disposition. Understand that *meekness* is not *weakness*. Untold multitudes have listened to the rhetoric of German philosopher Friedrich Nietzsche. One of his chief indictments against Christianity was that it lifts up those who humble themselves before others. Nietzsche glorified power and all expressions of it. "What is good?" he asked. "Everything that heightens the feeling of power in man, the will to power, power itself. What is bad? Everything that is born of weakness."[48] But what Nietzsche describes is contradictory! The strong man (i.e., smart, powerful, high-stationed, etc.) expressing his strength requires no strength at all. What makes him strong is his ability to push that nature aside and humbly give himself to his brothers, as Jesus suggested in Matthew 23:11 by saying, "The greatest among you will be your servant."

Jesus was the ultimate example of meekness. On the one hand, he stooped to wash his disciples' feet; on the other, he was in command of legions of angels that could wipe out the entire world in the blink of an eye. Meekness is demonstrated by extending love toward people. It's the mind-set of being teachable, submitting to authority, and submitting to leadership. Hear this: the attitude of humility is not just thinking less of yourself, but thinking of yourself less as you extend your energy to the benefit of those around you.[49]

Self-Control

Self-control is, simply, the ability to control yourself. It refers to how well an individual can keep him or herself in check, and to what degree they have mastery over their passions and appetites. Paul speaks of how we should control our bodies in 1 Corinthians 9:24–25: "Don't you know that the runners in a stadium all race, but only one receives the prize? Run in such a way to win the prize. Now everyone who competes exercises self-control in everything."

Remember, this is not a list of virtues for you to check off as you see them appear; rather, it is the fruit (singular) of the Spirit produced in us. When the Spirit dwells in a believer, he or she will display his fruit, just as Jesus did. Notice that Jesus displayed every single one of the fruits at all times during his ministry.

Since it is Christ's image into which we are being conformed, his fruit should be displayed. The only avenue for accomplishing this is through the Holy Spirit.

As a Christian, you should be constantly progressing closer to Christ than you were yesterday, last month, or last year. You should be extending kindness more today than you did last year. You should have more mastery over your faculties, desires, and passions than you did last month. You should have more peace with God than you had yesterday.

It is extraordinarily interesting that this passage describes these characteristics as fruit. Fruit is not meant to be consumed by the tree growing it. In the same way, the fruit you bear is not for you to consume, but for the benefit of those around you. Your self-control is not only for you; it's for your brother, your neighbor, your spouse. Your kindness is not just for you; it's for your children, your coworkers, strangers on the street. Your gentleness is not for you. Your patience is not for you. The fruit of the Spirit in your life is meant for a lost world around us dying to see the gospel manifested through us.

The Cultivation of Fruit

We explored first the battle that rages in the soul of every believer between the flesh and the spirit and how the blessings of walking in the Spirit aren't just for the person doing the walking. Finally, let us examine how we cultivate fruit in our lives.

In Galatians 5:24–25, Paul says something crucial to understanding how we cultivate fruit in our lives: "Now those who belong to Christ Jesus have crucified the flesh with its passions and desires. If we live by the Spirit, let us also keep in step with the Spirit." In this text, Paul's challenge to *crucify* the flesh is slightly different than his statement in Galatians 2:19–20, which says, "For through the law I died to the law, so that I might live for God. I have been crucified with Christ, and I no longer live, but Christ lives in me. The life I now live in the body, I live by faith in the Son of God." In this latter text, which is most often cited for crucifying the flesh, Paul speaks of a crucifixion that occurred in the past with Christ on the cross of Calvary—one that is already a spiritual reality in the life of a believer.

In Galatians 5:25 the emphasis is slightly different. The idea here is that we are to put to death the deeds of the flesh by our own actions. In his commentary on Galatians, Timothy George explains it this way, "Believers themselves are the agents of this crucifixion. Paul was here describing the process of mortification, the daily putting to death of the flesh through the disciplines of prayer, fasting, repentance, and self-control."[50] Jesus emphasized the same principle to his disciples in Luke 9 when he instructed them to deny themselves, take up their cross, and follow Him (Luke 9:23).

The Method

Crucifixion is, by its very nature, not an instantaneous occurrence; it brings about death over time. If Paul had been describing a process that were easy or quick, he may have said "behead the desires of the flesh," for beheading is quick and easy. Putting to death the desires of the flesh is, decidedly, not. I believe this is what Jesus envisioned when he mentioned taking up one's cross. Doing so was not instantaneous or easy, but could only be done through the strength he provides.

What does crucifying the flesh have to do with bearing fruit? The process outlines *how* we are to go about it. We bear fruit by keeping in step with the Spirit. Many of us have a difficult time keeping in step with the Spirit because our focus is elsewhere. We're either worried about running ahead or we're busy trying to catch up. The terminology Paul employs entreats us to walk *alongside* the Spirit, so that where he leads, we follow. Since you and I have been crucified in the past, it makes sense that we will daily crucify the flesh in the present.

Yesterday's crucifixion of the flesh is not sufficient for today's growth. It is absolutely crucial that the moment your feet hit the floor every day, you are actively, ruthlessly crucifying the flesh. I don't know about you, but some days when I wake up I feel as though the enemy is waiting at the edge of my bed. This makes it all the more crucial to constantly petition the Father, saying, "God, fill me with Your Spirit so that I can accomplish what you desire for me and resist the temptations of the evil one."

You cannot continue dabbling in sin if you wish to walk alongside the Spirit and bear fruit. So many people allow sin to fester in their midst and then wonder why they succumb to it so easily. We must constantly weed our spiritual gardens or the fruit of God will be choked out and our branches will not bear his fruit.

A Benefit for Others

Paul continues this thought in Galatians 5:26: "Let us not become conceited, provoking one another, envying one another." Conceit is the idea of being prideful or puffed up. A conceited person is one who is arrogant and boastful. John Stott said of this verse, "This is a very instructive verse because it shows that our conduct to others is determined by our opinion of ourselves."[51] As we examined when discussing the fruit of the Spirit, humility is not thinking less of yourself, it's not thinking of yourself at all!

Think of the outflow of the Spirit in believers' lives as unity among the body. Ephesians 5:18 says, "And don't get drunk with wine, which leads to reckless living, but be filled by the Spirit." Paul goes on to say in verses 19–21 when you're filled with the Spirit, something remarkable will happen in the body. As you yield to the spirit you will find yourself "speaking to one another in psalms, hymns, and spiritual songs, singing and making music with your heart to the Lord, giving thanks always for everything to God the Father in the name of our Lord Jesus Christ, submitting to one another in the fear of Christ."

The result of a spirit-filled life is that husbands will begin to love their wives as Christ loved the church. Wives will begin to lovingly submit to their husbands as the church submits to Christ. Children will begin to obey their parents. Employees will begin to respect their employers. What he's saying is that the way you treat others is the thermometer for the temperature of your heart with God. So how do you determine where your heart is? Ask those closest to you how you treat people. This exercise can be a tough pill to swallow. Ask your children if they think you respect your spouse by the way you talk to him or her. Ask your personal assistant who works with you in the office how you treat people and how you speak to other people.

It will be an eye-opener for some. Are you patient? Are you compassionate? Do you display kindness, goodness, and self-control? Would your closest friends say the way you treat people is the outflow of a heart completely in tune with God, producing the fruit of God? Paul tells us the fruit of the Spirit is available to us if we submit to the Lord, allowing ourselves to be ruled by him, consumed by him, and controlled by him. You simply have to make the choice. Are you going to yield to the flesh or to the Spirit?

Hudson Taylor's Spiritual Secret

In the book *Hudson Taylor's Spiritual Secret*, we see that Hudson's spiritual life reached a turning point when he understood the purpose of abiding in Christ. God used a letter from a friend to open his eyes to the secret of prospering in the Christian life. He described this secret like this:

> To let my loving Savior work in me His will, my sanctification, is what I would live for by His grace. Abiding, not striving nor struggling; looking often unto Him; trusting Him for present power . . . resting in the love of an almighty Savior, in the joy of a complete salvation, "free from all sin"—this is not new, and yet it is new to me. I feel as though the dawning of a glorious day had risen upon me. I hail it with trembling, yet with trust. I seem to have got to the edge only, but of a boundless sea; to have sipped only, but of that which fully satisfies. Christ literally all seems to me, now, the power, the only power for service, the only ground for unchanging joy. . . . Not a striving to have faith . . . but a looking off to the Faithful One seems all we need; a resting in the Loved One entirely, for time and for eternity.[52]

Abiding in Christ is a slow-moving process. But don't be discouraged. The slowest-growing trees sometimes bear the sweetest fruit.

Chapter 8

THE FRUIT OF PRAISE

Unending Worship

When I was growing up in New Orleans, I wanted to be like Mike. Every afternoon after school, I would press play on my parents' VCR to watch *Michael Jordan's Playground* with basketball in hand. When Mike performed a move, I would press pause, run outside, and as best as a 6'6" uncoordinated white boy could, I would imitate his movements. It worked at home, or so I imagined. It didn't work so well in games.

Off the court, I don't mimic Michael Jordan's actions, but I do think of the men who invested in me. I think of their examples often: how they've lived, how they've taught, how they've ministered to people, how they've preached the Word, and how they've loved.

In fact, every one of us is following something or someone. We have all had teachers and role models, leaders and coaches. We've all wanted to be like somebody else at one point or another, even if it wasn't necessarily a conscious decision. We must, then, be very careful, or else we will be following false teachers or worldly influences without even realizing it.

Fortunately, we have a system of checks and balances to ensure our feet are following the correct path. We've been given an example in Jesus Christ to live by.

Imitable Faith

The writer of Hebrews wraps up the book with a series of extremely practical exhortations. Hebrews 13:7–8 says, "*Remember* your leaders, who have spoken God's word to you. As you carefully observe the outcome of their lives, *imitate* their faith. Jesus Christ is the same yesterday, today, and forever" (emphasis mine). The two key words in this text are the main verbs: *remember* and *imitate*. Paul actually used the same verb for *"remember"* in 2 Timothy 2:8, when he said, "*Remember* Jesus Christ, risen from the dead and descended from David" (emphasis mine). *Remembering* is more than just thinking about something. What both Paul and the writer of Hebrews are getting at is the idea of pondering and meditating—carefully considering the role your leaders have played in your life.

"Your leaders," to the writer of Hebrews, means those who have invested in you through the preaching and teaching of the Word of God. These could be like the shepherds and teachers mentioned by Paul in Ephesians 4.

What Hebrews describes is not just a relationship through which you have passively learned something, but a *discipleship* relationship in which someone has led you to become more Christlike. The leaders here didn't just teach their philosophy or particular worldview, they taught the *Word of God*! So when we are instructed to remember our teachers, we are to remember and ponder their example, their instruction, and the One toward whom they were leading us: Jesus Christ himself.

Imitate is the second command the writer offers. It is not a passive command to sit and think, it requires replicating what has been modeled for us. "Take it all in," the writer may as well be saying, "because soon you're going to be asked to repeat their example." This was exactly the way *Michael Jordan's Playground* worked in my life. It displayed M.J.'s moves in a way that encouraged me to emulate and imitate them on the court. With careful consideration of M.J.'s footwork and ball-handling skills, I would be able to reproduce his skills in the game. At least, that was the plan. (Unfortunately, the lack of skill in executing these moves in district games was the culprit for bench riding.)

The same principle is true in our spiritual lives. As a disciple who makes disciples, you won't only be looking to the example of others; others will also be looking to your example. It eliminates the possibility of saying, "I don't care what people think about what I'm doing. I'm not hurting anybody but myself by living this way." The instruction by the author of Hebrews takes that mentality to task by saying you're hurting *everyone* around you by sinning—those who know you well and those who don't. If you claim allegiance to Christ, there will be people watching you, whether you like it or not.

Consider Hebrews 13 again. Verse 7 tells us the thing we are to imitate is the faith of our leaders. A very succinct definition of faith is *trust and belief in God that results in action.* Those who are familiar with Hebrews know that chapter 13 is only two chapters after one of the greatest treatments of faith in all of Scripture, so when the writer mentions *faith*, he has in mind the previous chapter.

In Hebrews 11, the author lists what is often called the "Hall of Faith." Included in the list are men and women who spoke the Word of God without apology, followed God obediently, and gave their lives willingly to the cause of Christ. Every record of faith in the chapter is accompanied by an action:

- Abel offered a sacrifice to God.
- Noah built an ark.
- Abraham went out in the face of uncertainty.
- Sarah bore a child in her old age.
- Moses' parents hid him for three months despite the king's edict.
- Rahab gave a friendly welcome to the spies.

Faith is not a passive, mental assent; it will be accompanied with action to be called faith. James 2:17 calls faith that isn't accompanied by action "dead." This is why we are instructed in Hebrews 13:7 to imitate the faith of our teachers—because faith is reproducible.

Discipling Relationships

There are three relationships every believer should foster: a "Paul," a "Barnabas," and a "Timothy." A "Paul" is a spiritual father, one who is more mature than you are in his faith and pours into you from that place. A "Timothy" is the person in whom you are investing. The gospel you have received and the faith you possess is not for your benefit only. A "Timothy" is somebody who could call you their Paul. You are actively investing in this person. A "Barnabas" is a peer who is in your life to sharpen your faith, for "iron sharpens iron, and one person sharpens another" (Prov. 27:17). This person is in the same walk of life as you and can offer both encouragement and stability to your Christian journey.

If you cannot recall someone by name who fits each of these three categories, don't be alarmed—there is no time better to start than now! The D-Group (discipleship group), as we call them, is a gender-exclusive group of three to five people who meet together at least once a week for a minimum of a year. Relationships for these smaller groups are more formal than in a Sunday school class or Life Group. Because of the intimate setting, participants will see personal, rapid spiritual growth as a result. (I'll talk more about this in a moment.)

Some of you may find yourself saying, "I don't have a mentor or an example to follow." Yes you do. In a world where leaders come and go, Jesus Christ—the only one who will never let you down—is our ultimate example. After a lengthy bibliography of the faithful men and women in Hebrews 11, the author states:

> Therefore, since we also have such a large cloud of witnesses surrounding us, let us lay aside every hindrance and the sin that so easily ensnares us. Let us run with endurance the race that lies before us, keeping our eyes on Jesus, the source and perfecter of our faith. For the joy that lay before him, he endured the cross, despising the shame, and sat down at the right hand of the throne of God. (Heb. 12:1–3)

The most important discipleship model is Jesus. Open the Old Testament and sense the anticipation of his arrival. Open the New Testament and drink richly from the well of his life. Imitate his actions and model his pattern of living. He is our supreme mentor.

This section may seem out of place in a conversation about spiritual examples, but it is actually crucial. As we engage in discipleship, the purpose is to move in the same direction as those with whom we're traveling: toward Jesus. The way we grow toward him is by following his example and by using close relationships around us to hold us accountable to continue drawing near to him. Furthermore, we depend on a relationship with Christ and with his Spirit to have a solid under-standing of his Word, lest we be led astray by false teaching. Pray for God to bring a Paul into your life. Then go ask for someone to invest in you. You'll be sur-prised by who will say yes.

Defying False Doctrine

The author of Hebrews continues by offering a warning:

> Don't be led astray by various kinds of strange teachings; for it is good for the heart to be estab-lished by grace and not by food regulations, since those who observe them have not ben-efited. We have an altar from which those who worship at the tabernacle do not have a right to eat. For the bodies of those animals whose blood is brought into the most holy place by the high priest as a sin offering are burned outside the camp. (Heb. 13:9–11)

The imperative "don't be led astray" connects this section to the previous one, which encouraged us to cultivate godly relationships. By fostering gospel-cen-tered friendships with other believers through Life Groups and D-Groups, we will simultaneously avoid strange teaching. "To be led astray" means to be car-ried off or misled. The word picture being portrayed here is that of a river carrying something away down-stream. Additionally, it is a picture of an undiscipled person who is confused by every stray current, or off-shoot of unorthodox doctrine.

It is unfortunate that some Christians are illiterate when it comes to the Word of God. Many of us, includ-ing myself, have family members and close friends who are constantly questioning Christianity as a result of scriptural immaturity. "Wasn't Jesus married to Mary

Magdalene?" "Doesn't Jesus want you to be rich and healthy?" "Isn't it true that Mary wasn't actually a *virgin* and that word just means 'young girl'?" The abundance of false doctrine floating around today is staggering. This is why it is absolutely crucial for us to root our faith in what is sound and true—so we will not be "blown around by every wind of teaching" (Eph. 4:14).

In Hebrews 13:9, the doctrine the author is imparting is that the cross of Christ is the once-and-for-all sacrifice for all of mankind. Notice verse 10: "We have an altar from which those who worship at the tabernacle do not have a right to eat." The word *altar* in verse 10 is a term that symbolically represents the cross of Christ. Six times in the book of Hebrews,[53] Jesus Christ is pointed to as the final sacrifice for humanity, and the phrase "We have an altar" symbolizes the redemption we experience through his death.

What is the point of not being able to eat food? In order to understand this, we must first understand the process of atonement in Hebraic law.

Atonement

The Jewish people would bring their sacrifices to the temple by slaying an animal outside of the camp and disposing of its carcass before bringing its blood as an offering to splatter on the altar.

On the Day of Atonement, a weightier act took place. For six days, every day, the high priest would cleanse himself in preparation for the big day. Then on the seventh day, the Day of Atonement (Yom Kippur), the high priest would rise and ceremonially cleanse himself again before making a sacrificial offering for himself and his household. Next, he would take two goats for two different purposes: one as a sin offering and the other as a *scapegoat*. He offered one goat as an offering to atone for the sin of the people, but the scapegoat was different. The priest would lay his hands on the goat's head and spiritually "transpose" the sin of the people onto it. He then handed the goat off to a priest who was responsible for leading it into the wilderness.

This is what the author of Hebrews has in mind. The entire system, according to the writer, is broken and temporary. The Jews of the day were saying, "Okay, we believe in Jesus, but we still need to sacrifice animals to God." The author makes clear that if you still live under the old Levitical system, you have to play by the rules of the system, which doesn't offer a once-and-for-all sacrifice. The whole reason for the sacrifice in the first place was to foreshadow the sacrifice to come—Jesus Christ. Praise God we have one who went *outside the camp*, where the sacrifices were burned and where the unclean resided, so that we may live *inside* the camp!

The author of Hebrews continues: "Therefore, Jesus also suffered outside the gate, so that he might sanctify the people by his own blood" (Heb. 13:12). Pay close attention to this question: Why did Jesus have to go outside the camp? Numbers 5 details the instructions God gave to His people concerning those who were "outside the camp":

> The LORD instructed Moses: "Command the Israelites to send away anyone from the camp who is afflicted with a skin disease, anyone who has a discharge, or anyone who is defiled because of a corpse. Send away both male or female; send them outside the camp, so that they will not defile their camps where I dwell among them." The Israelites did this, sending them outside the camp. The Israelites did as the LORD instructed Moses. (vv. 1–4)

In light of this text, imagine you have a friend or a family member who comes down with a head-to-toe skin disease. What is the prescribed response, according to Numbers 5? They are expelled. They didn't do anything to contract the disease. Still, they are sent away, alone. They are isolated from the people of God inside the camp.

In a ritual sense, these people are sinful and unclean. But have they really done anything wrong? Why would God do this to people who were, at least partially, innocent? You have to understand that in a day and age with no antibiotics, God's system for preserving the whole nation was to quarantine the individual. It may seem at times like the commands of God are harsh, but do not miss his reasoning. God's commands are always right and are always gracious toward his people. They are for protection, not mere punishment.

Notice Numbers 5:3 again: "Send away both male or female; send them outside the camp." Why? "So that they will not defile their camps where I dwell among them." Since God is in the camp, no defilement can be present. It's what happened to Adam and Eve once they became tarnished and defiled: they were sent out from the garden where God dwelt with them. They were separated from his presence.

This notion of separation is serious business to God. He forbade the well from touching the sick with leprosy, dead bodies, and people with bodily discharges. Consider other such mandates in Leviticus 13 and 15:

> The person who has a case of serious skin disease is to have his clothes torn and his hair hanging loose, and he must cover his mouth and cry out, 'Unclean, unclean!' He will remain unclean as long as he has the disease; he is

unclean. He must live alone in a place outside the camp. (Lev. 13:45–46)

The LORD spoke to Moses and Aaron: "Speak to the Israelites and tell them: When any man has a discharge from his member, he is unclean. This is uncleanness of his discharge: Whether his member secretes the discharge or retains it, he is unclean. All the days that his member secretes or retains anything because of his discharge, he is unclean. Any bed the man with the discharge lies on will be unclean, and any furniture he sits on will be unclean. Anyone who touches his bed is to wash his clothes and bathe with water, and he will remain unclean until evening. Whoever sits on furniture that the man with the discharge was sitting on is to wash his clothes and bathe with water, and he will remain unclean until evening. Whoever touches the body of the man with a discharge is to wash his clothes and bathe with water, and he will remain unclean until evening. If the man with the discharge spits on anyone who is clean, he is to wash his clothes and bathe with water, and he will remain unclean until evening."' (Lev. 15:1–8)

Every person a defiled person touched became unclean. Why in the world does God devote so many chapters in the Old Testament to defilement, particularly in the book of Leviticus? He illustrates his point that physical defilement points us to the spiritual defilement within each of us. We clearly need someone to clean us up.

The One Who Cleans Us Up

We know that every law, even the laws regarding physical defilement, point to Jesus. In Luke 24, on the road to Emmaus, Jesus led a Bible study with two disciples. Starting with Moses and the prophets, he showed how all the Old Testament pointed to him. Can you imagine having a seat at the table for that Bible study? It was the greatest home group ever held by anyone to walk the face of the earth, and the entire point was to reveal how everything in the Old Testament pointed to him.

This same emphasis is seen in the three healings in Luke's gospel. In Luke 5 (remember, Luke is a physician), the author identifies three cases of physical disease with perfect clarity: a leper, someone with bodily discharge, and a little girl who has died. Luke 5:12–13 records:

> While he was in one of the towns, a man was there who had leprosy all over him. He saw Jesus, fell facedown, and begged him: "Lord, if you are willing, you can make me clean." Reaching out his hand, Jesus touched him, saying, "I am willing; be made clean," and immediately the leprosy left him.

Can you hear the crowd behind Jesus as this unclean man is trying to touch him? Every one of them knows the rules for what happens if you contact someone with a serious skin disease, so they are all probably yelling, "Don't you know who this man is? Don't even come near him; don't even touch him! You'll get expelled, rejected, sent away!" Disregarding the crowd's insistence, with no fear of being sent away, Jesus reached out, touched the man, and watched the disease leave his body—all while remaining clean himself.

Luke 8:42–44 records another encounter:

While he was going, the crowds were nearly crushing him. A woman suffering from bleeding for twelve years, who had spent all she had on doctors and yet could not be healed by any, approached from behind and touched the end of his robe. Instantly her bleeding stopped.

Can you picture the crowds again here? They would be running far away from this woman, giving her space as they passed her on the street. *Don't let her touch you!* they are thinking. Listen to Jesus's response:

"Who touched Me?" Jesus asked. When they all denied it, Peter said, "Master, the crowds are hemming you in and pressing against you." "Someone did touch me," said Jesus. "I know that power has gone out from me." When the woman saw that she was discovered, she came trembling and fell down before him. In the presence of all the people, she declared the reason she had touched him and how she was instantly healed. "Daughter," he said to her, "your faith has saved you. Go in peace." (Luke 8:45–48)

This woman's faith in Jesus as the Messiah made her clean. Do you remember the requirements for those who were unclean in Leviticus? Being quarantined from everybody else brought shame and loneliness, and this woman had been outside the camp for twelve years. Imagine twelve years of isolation and depression, and the first word you hear from the One who welcomed you is, "Daughter."

We have one final encounter in the same chapter:

While he was still speaking, someone came from the synagogue leader's house and said, "Your daughter is dead. Don't bother the teacher any-more." When Jesus heard it, he answered him, "Don't be afraid. Only believe, and she will be saved." After he came to the house, he let no one enter with him except Peter, John, James, and the child's father and mother. Everyone was crying and mourning for her. But he said, "Stop crying, because she is not dead but asleep." They laughed at him, because they knew she was dead. So he took her by the hand and called out, "Child, get up!" Her spirit returned, and she got up at once. Then he gave orders that she be given something to eat. Her parents were astounded. (Luke 8:49–56)

"Don't touch that dead girl, Jesus! You'll defile yourself and be forced out of the camp!" And yet Jesus explicitly reached out, took the girl's hand, and breathed into her the breath of life. She becomes clean again; he remains clean.

The Clean Among the Filthy

Touching this leprous man, this unclean woman, and this dead girl should have made Jesus unclean as well, yet it didn't. He accomplished what the cer-emonial law couldn't do: make someone clean or whole again. The law could outline what to do in the event that someone becomes unclean, and it could tell you what to do once you became clean again, but nowhere did it explain, explicitly, the solution for becoming clean. Only one person can make someone clean: Jesus Christ, who is the fulfillment of those laws.

How could Jesus touch someone who was unclean and remain clean himself? The priests couldn't do it, Moses couldn't do it, the prophets couldn't do it, the high priest couldn't do it. Hear this: *only* God can do it—this proves that Jesus *is* God.

What gives Jesus the right to heal our sickness without being defiled? Look back at Hebrews 13:11–13:

> For the bodies of those animals whose blood is brought into the most holy place by the high priest as a sin offering are burned outside the camp. Therefore, Jesus also suffered outside the gate, so that he might sanctify the people by his own blood. Let us then go to him outside the camp, bearing his disgrace.

Jesus knew the only way those outside the camp would be able to live inside the camp was if someone bore their reproach. Another way to say that Jesus "went outside" would be to say he was cut off completely. There was never a time when Jesus was not one with the Father, *except* on the cross of Calvary when he cried out with a loud voice, "My God, my God, why have you forsaken me?" (Matt. 27:46 ESV).

I imagine he went to the Father and said something along these lines: "I know the only way people will not be cut off forever is if I'm cut off for them, so I'll do it. I'll bear their reproach. I'll take their sin. I'll go outside the camp for them." (Hebrews 13:11–13 makes the connection of "going outside the camp" to Leviticus 16.) You have to understand how great the sacrifice Jesus made was; he literally severed himself from the Father so that you and I don't have to be.

After it was finished, we didn't hear, "My Son bless you and keep you. May My face shine upon You." No, we heard instead judgment and cursing: "My wrath be upon You!" The Son did not experience perfect peace with his Father; he absorbed the horror of hell for us. Jesus lived the life we couldn't live, and died a death we should have died.

Have you ever noticed why Jesus was crucified outside of the city of Jerusalem on a small hill? Why didn't they just beat him in Pilate's palace and then stick his cross in the ground right there for everyone to see? Why did he have to walk the Via Dolorosa, outside the city, and then be strung up facing it? Because *that's where we were.*

He went outside to meet us where we were, in the wake of the wrath of God. He went outside the camp so that you and I can live inside the camp for all of eternity. He was cut off for *you* so that you would never be cut off from him. He can touch any defilement and make it clean. He can touch any brokenness in your life and make it whole. He can take any hurt from your past and make it right—and he demands only one thing for it: Praise.

A Praise Habit

Perhaps the reason people don't praise God unceasingly or proclaim his gospel to the ends of the world unapologetically is because they have a misunderstanding of the magnitude of what he accomplished. If we don't have a proper view of who God is, how he made himself known to us, and what he desires from us in return, we won't partake of the final aspect of the text.

Let us then go to him outside the camp, bearing his disgrace. For we do not have an enduring city here; instead, we seek the one to come. Therefore, through him let us continually offer up to God a sacrifice of praise, that is, the fruit of lips that confess his name. Don't neglect to do what is good and to share, for God is pleased with such sacrifices. (Heb. 13:13–16)

The author expects us to offer a sacrifice of praise. We should continually, without ceasing, remember who God is, what God did, and what God will do. Day by day, hour by hour, moment by moment, our lips are to be full of God's praise.

When praise becomes a habit, your actions will change as well. Sitting idly is not an option—we're called to go out.

If you want to be where Jesus is, you have to go where Jesus went. Do you know where he is? He's outside the camp. He's among the sick and the weak. He's among those who live in constant terror from enemies. He's among the hurting and the diseased. He's among the sinners and the addicts. Are we somehow excluded from the places Jesus visited—outside the camp, outside of our comfort zones, outside of the conveniences we have on the inside—for the glory of God?

Two months after losing everything in Hurricane Katrina, I had a trip scheduled to Indonesia with David Platt and Rob Wilton. I told Kandi, my wife, "I probably shouldn't go on the trip. I should stay home with you." She graciously responded, "No, Robby. God has led you to go on this trip. You need to go." Knowing full well how unwise it is to disregard the direction of both God and my wife, I went.

I would have missed a spiritual marker in my life had I not gone. We flew into Indonesia, which has 237 million people, 88 percent of whom are Muslim—and 15 percent of those are militant. We went there to teach in a Christian seminary. It was hardly safe, but it was incredibly rewarding.

We noticed that a huge number of people showed up at the training, despite the constant threats from their Muslim countrymen (some of whom wanted to kill them for their beliefs). They came by bus, by motorcycle, by foot. Some rode three deep on a motorbike for days to hear us teach them how to teach and study the Word of God. At the end of the training, I told Rob, "We have taught them all week. I want to hear *their* stories." So we handed them the microphone on the final day. For hours we listened to testimonies about the cost of converting to Christianity.

We heard about their homes being decimated after professing faith in Christ. We heard about their churches being bombed and burned down. We heard about countless death threats. We listened to one woman share her testimony about how her father beat her repeatedly with a chair to the point of death for leaving Islam. We heard of brothers losing their lives.

The event culminated with David Platt, who was given the honor of speaking at their graduation ceremony. Now, graduating from this seminary was quite different than graduating from an American seminary. Not only do they have to go through all of the schooling necessary to receive a seminary degree, they were required to plant a church in a Muslim community and witness five baptized believers before walking.

Here we were, three American seminary-trained men, sitting with models of fearless faith, feeling inadequate and humbled. We sat speechless as we heard of two of their fellow classmates who died in the process of planting the church required for their graduation.

That day, I realized Jesus Christ expects us to follow his example and go outside of the camp to the hard places. He wants us to go outside of our comfort zones, into the jungles of Ecuador, to the Ivory Coast of Africa, to the center of the bomb-ravaged Middle East.

And we are to do it with *joy*! It's where our King went, and we have the privilege of following him. We go because we believe Jesus can cleanse anyone of anything. We go because Jesus Christ is worthy of all our worship and all their worship.

Bearing Much Fruit

My hope for you is that you will continue to grow in your spiritual journey long after you read this book. I pray your roots are planted firmly like a tree between two streams, and your life bears the fruit of someone who has been bought at a great price—and will continue to bear fruit for many years to come. Since the foundation for Christian living is the knowledge of God, I want to use this as an opportunity to encourage you to continue. The books in the Growing Up Series are merely the beginning of your journey; what you *do* with what they say is the most important part. People often take an enthusiastic first step, only to backslide from a lack of direction. After you take your first step, you need to find ways to keep your momentum up so you can continue to passionately pursue Christ.

The Disciplemaking Pathway is a simple, reproducible process for growing in your relationship with God (see replicate.org for more information). Keep in mind that a growing disciple of Christ should be engaged in all three groups within the pathway.

The first step is to make a commitment to attend a weekly church gathering, called the *Congregation*. The weekly gathering of believers is crucial, for it affords you time to commune with a body of people united with the same aim: to worship God through hearing his Word and singing the praise of his name. But it cannot stop here. Meeting once a week with believers is a great start, but when constantly bombarded by the forces of the world trying to drag everything you gain on Sundays out of you, you need more.

This is why the second step of the Disciplemaking Pathway is the *Life Group*, or the *Community*. We call it a Life Group rather than Sunday school, because it is much more than another opportunity to passively take in information in a large-group setting. You are a community together—a small group of people in similar stations of life, learning the Word of God and living life together. A Life Group facilitates discussion which cannot take place among the Congregation because of its size. The most exciting part of the Life Group is that it is the fishing pond out of which D-Groups are formed.

The final step of the Disciplemaking Pathway is the *D-Group*, or the *Core*. A D-Group is a single-sex group of three to five individuals who meet weekly (at least) for the purpose of accountability, Scripture memory, in-depth Bible study, and brotherly or sisterly growth alongside others who pursue the face and character of Christ.

I am confident that he who began this good work in you will bring it to completion at the day of the Lord Jesus Christ. He is perfect, good, and incomparably loving. Take today as the first day of the rest of your spiritual journey toward becoming more like the One who saved you.

Appendix

FOUNDATIONS 260 (F260)

One of the most important aspects of the disciple's life is Bible intake. Reading, meditating, and responding to the Word of God is vital to every believer. This has a direct correlation to the fruit that the disciple bears. We want to get into the Word of God until the Word gets into us. The more we know about God, the more we love him, and the more we love him, the more we will obey him.

The following Bible reading plan is called Foundations 260, or F260 for short. It is a one-year plan intended to provide an overview of the Bible. The plan offers five days' worth of reading per week with a couple of chapters each day. The design of the F260 is intended to help busy believers stay consistent in reading and studying the Word of God.

Please utilize the F260 plan, or another helpful Bible reading plan, in your personal devotional time, or in your D-Group. As you get into the Word individually and in a group, God will use it to help you bear fruit.

Week 1
Genesis 1–2
Genesis 3–4
Genesis 6–7
Genesis 8–9
Job 1–2
Memory Verses:
Genesis 1:27
Hebrews 11:7

Week 2
Job 38–39
Job 40–42
Genesis 11–12
Genesis 15
Genesis 16–17
Memory Verses:
Hebrews 11:8–
10; 11:6

Week 3
Genesis 18–19
Genesis 20–21
Genesis 22
Genesis 24
Genesis 25:19–
34; 26
Memory Verses:
Romans 4:20–
22; Hebrews
11:17–19

Week 4
Genesis 27–28
Genesis
29–30:24
Genesis 31–32
Genesis 33; 35
Genesis 37
Memory Verses:
2 Corinthians

10:12; 1 John
3:18

Week 5
Genesis 39–40
Genesis 41
Genesis 42–43
Genesis 44–45
Genesis 46–47
Memory Verses:
Ephesians
3:20–21; Romans
8:28–30

Week 6
Genesis 48–49
Genesis 50
Exodus 1
Exodus 2–3
Exodus 4–5
Exodus 6–7
Memory Verses:
Genesis 50:20;
Hebrews
11:24–26

Week 7
Exodus 8–9
Exodus 10–11
Exodus 12
Exodus 13:17–14
Exodus 16–17
Memory Verses:
John 1:29;
Hebrews 9:22

Week 8
Exodus
19–20 Ten
Commandments
Exodus 24–25

Exodus 26–27
Tabernacle
Exodus 28–29
Tabernacle
Exodus 30–31
Tabernacle
*Memory
Verses:* Ten
Commandments

Week 9
Exodus 32–33
Exodus 34–36:1
Exodus 40
Leviticus 8–9
Leviticus 16–17
Memory Verses:
Exodus 33:16;
Matthew
22:37–39

Week 10
Leviticus 23
Leviticus 26
Numbers 11–12
Numbers 13–14
Numbers 16–17
Memory Verses:
Leviticus 26:13;
Deuteronomy
31:7–8

Week 11
Numbers 20;
27:12–23
Numbers 34–35
Deuteronomy
1–2
Deuteronomy
3–4
Deuteronomy
6–7

Memory Verses:
Deuteronomy
4:7; 6:4–9

Week 12
Deuteronomy
8–9
Deuteronomy
30–31
Deuteronomy
32:48–52; 34
Joshua 1–2
Joshua 3–4
Memory Verses:
Joshua 1:8–9;
Psalm 1:1–2

Week 13
Joshua 5:10–15;
6
Joshua 7–8
Joshua 23–24
Judges 2–3
Judges 4
Memory Verses:
Joshua 24:14–15;
Judges 2:12

Week 14
Judges 6–7
Judges 13–14
Judges 15–16
Ruth 1–2
Ruth 3–4
Memory Verses:
Galatians 4:4–5;
Psalm 19:14

Week 15
1 Samuel 1–2
1 Samuel 3; 8
1 Samuel 9–10

1 Samuel 13–14
1 Samuel 15–16
Memory Verses:
1 Samuel 15:22;
16:7

Week 16
1 Samuel 17–18
1 Samuel 19–20
1 Samuel 21–22
Psalm 22;
1 Samuel
24–25:1
1 Samuel 28; 31
Memory Verses:
1 Samuel
17:46–47;
2 Timothy 4:17

Week 17
2 Samuel 1;
2:1–7
2 Samuel 3:1; 5;
Psalm 23
2 Samuel 6–7
Psalm 18
2 Samuel 9
2 Samuel 11–12
Memory Verses:
Psalms 23:1–3;
51:10–1

Week 18
Psalm 51
2 Samuel 24;
Psalm 24
Psalms 1; 19
Psalms 103;
119:1–48
Psalm
119:49–128

Memory Verses:
Psalms 1:1–7;
119:7–11

Week 19
Psalms 119:129–
176; 139
Psalms 148–150
1 Kings 2
1 Kings 3; 6
1 Kings 8; 9:1–9
Memory Verses:
Psalms 139:1–3;
139:15–16

Week 20
Proverbs 1–2
Proverbs 3–4
Proverbs 16–18
Proverbs 31
1 Kings 11–12
Memory Verses:
Proverbs 1:7;
3:5–6

Week 21
1 Kings 16:29–
34; 17
1 Kings 18–19
1 Kings 21–22
2 Kings 2
2 Kings 5; 6:1–23
Memory Verses:
Psalm 63:1;
17:15

Week 22
Jonah 1–2
Jonah 3–4
Hosea 1–3
Amos 1:1; 9
Joel 1–3

Memory Verses:
Psalm 16:11;
John 11:25–26

Week 23
Isaiah 6; 9
Isaiah 44–45
Isaiah 52–53
Isaiah 65–66
Micah 1; 4:6–13;
5
Memory Verses:
Isaiah 53:5–6;
1 Peter 2:23–24

Week 24
2 Kings 17–18
2 Kings 19–21
2 Kings 22–23
Jeremiah 1–3:5
Jeremiah 25; 29
Memory Verses:
Proverbs 29:18;
Jeremiah 1:15

Week 25
Jeremiah 31:31–
40; 32–33
Jeremiah 52;
2 Kings 24–25
Ezekiel 1:1–3;
36:16–38; 37
Daniel 1–2
Daniel 3
Memory Verses:
Ezekiel 36:26–
27; Psalm 51:10

Week 26
Daniel 5–6
Daniel 9–10; 12
Ezra 1–2

Ezra 3–4
Ezra 5–6
Memory Verses:
Daniel 6:26–27;
9:19

Week 27
Zechariah 1:1–6;
2; 12
Ezra 7–8
Ezra 9–10
Esther 1–2
Esther 3–4
Memory Verses:
Zephaniah 3:17;
1 Peter 3:15

Week 28
Esther 5–7
Esther 8–10
Nehemiah 1–2
Nehemiah 3–4
Nehemiah 5–6
Memory Verses:
Deuteronomy
29:29; Psalms
101:3–4

Week 29
Nehemiah 7–8
Nehemiah 9
Nehemiah 10
Nehemiah 11
Nehemiah 12
Memory Verses:
Nehemiah 9:6;
Colossians
1:15–16

Week 30
Nehemiah 13
Malachi 1

Malachi 2
Malachi 3
Malachi 4
Memory Verses:
Psalm 51:17;
Colossians
1:19–20

Week 31
Luke 1
Luke 2
Matthew 1–2
Mark 1
John 1
Memory Verses:
John 1:1–2; 14

Week 32
Matthew 2–4
Matthew 5
Matthew 6
Matthew 7
Matthew 8
Memory Verses:
Matthew 5:16;
6:33

Week 33
Luke 9:10–62
Mark 9–10
Luke 12
John 3–4
Luke 14
Memory Verses:
Luke 14:26–27;
14:33

Week 34
John 6
Matthew
19:16–30
Luke 15–16

Luke 17:11–37;
18
Mark 10
Memory Verses:
Mark 10:45;
John 6:37

Week 35
John 11;
Matthew
21:1–13
John 13
John 14–15
John 16
Matthew 24
Memory Verses:
John 13:34–35;
15:4–5

Week 36
Matthew
24:1–46
John 17
Matthew 26:47;
27:31
Matthew
27:32–66; Luke
23:26–56
John 19
Memory Verses:
Luke 23:34; John
17:3

Week 37
Mark 16;
Matthew 28
Luke 24
John 20–21
Matthew 28
Acts 1

Memory Verses:
Matthew
28:18–20
Acts 1:8

Week 38
Acts 2–3
Acts 4–5
Acts 6
Acts 7
Acts 8–9
Memory Verses:
Acts 2:42; 4:31

Week 39
Acts 10–11
Acts 12
Acts 13–14
James 1–2
James 3–5
Memory Verses:
James 1: 2–4;
2:17

Week 40
Acts 15–16
Galatians 1–3
Galatians 4–6
Acts 17–18:17
1 Thessalonians
1–2
Memory Verses:
Acts 17:11;
17:24–25

Week 41
1 Thessalonians
3–5
2 Thessalonians
1–3
Acts 18–19

1 Corinthians
1–2
1 Corinthians
3–4
Memory Verses:
1 Corinthians
1:18;
1 Thessalonians
5:23–24

Week 42
1 Corinthians
4–5
1 Corinthians
6–7
1 Corinthians
8–9
1 Corinthians
10–11
1 Corinthians
12–14
Memory Verses:
1 Corinthians
10:13; 13:13

Week 43
1 Corinthians
15–16
2 Corinthians
1–2
2 Corinthians
3–4
2 Corinthians
5–6
2 Corinthians
7–8
Memory Verses:
Romans 1:16–17;
1 Corinthians
15:3–4

Week 44
2 Corinthians
9–10
2 Corinthians
11–13
Romans 1–2;
Acts 20:1–3
Romans 3–4
Romans 5–6
Memory Verses:
Romans 4:20–22;
5:1

Week 45
Romans 7–8
Romans 9–10
Romans 11–12
Romans 13–14
Romans 15–16
Memory Verses:
Romans 8:1;
12:1–2

Week 46
Acts 20–21
Acts 22–23
Acts 24–25
Acts 26–27
Acts 28
Memory Verses:
Acts 20:24;
2 Corinthians
4:7–10

Week 47
Colossians 1–2
Colossians 3–4
Ephesians 1–2
Ephesians 3–4
Ephesians 5–6

Memory Verses:
Ephesians 2:8–
10; Colossians
2:6–7

Week 48
Philippians 1–2
Philippians 3–4
Hebrews 1–2
Hebrews 3–4
Hebrews 5–6
Memory Verses:
Philippians
3:7–8; Hebrews
4:14–16

Week 49
Hebrews 6–7
Hebrews 8–9
Hebrews 10
Hebrew 11
Hebrews 12
Memory Verses:
Galatians
2:19–20;
2 Corinthians
5:17

Week 50
1 Timothy 1–3
1 Timothy 4–6
2 Timothy 1–2
2 Timothy 3–4
1 Peter 1–2
Memory Verses:
2 Timothy 2:1–2;
2:15

Week 51
1 Peter 3–4
1 Peter 5;
1 John 1

1 John 2–3
1 John 4–5
Revelation 1
Memory Verses:
1 Peter 2:11;
1 John 4:10–11

Week 52
Revelation 2
Revelation 3
Revelation
19:6–20
Revelation 21
Revelation 22
Memory Verses:
Revelation 3:19;
21:3–4

ACKNOWLEDGMENTS

I'm grateful for the efforts of many who helped make this work a reality. Tim LaFleur, Dave Wiley, Mollie Wiley, Paul Laso, Kandi Gallaty, Gus Hernandez, and Chris Swain offered constructive criticism to make this book stronger. I couldn't have finished this project without your input and support. You worked tirelessly to assist me in making the deadline for publication.

I am grateful for the editorial insights from Hamilton Barber and Chris Swain who shaped this book into what it is today. Thanks for going above and beyond to help complete the work.

I am thankful for my wife, Kandi, and my boys, Rig and Ryder, who encouraged me every step of the way. Kandi, your example in making disciples inspires me to be a better disciplemaker.

Last but not least, I am eternally grateful for the salvation I have in Christ. Even though it's been fourteen years since I first met the Lord, I've never gotten over being saved. My prayer is that many people will bear much fruit for the kingdom.

NOTES

1. Herman Bavinck, *Our Reasonable Faith* (Grand Rapids, MI: Wm. B. Eerdmans Publishing Co., 1956), 475.

2. The *Old Farmer's Almanac*, http://www.alamanac.com/plant/grapes. Accessed January 20, 2017.

3. Ibid.

4. Ibid.

5. Ibid.

6. William Nicholson, *Shadowlands*. Directed by Richard Attenborough, New York: HBO, 1993.

7. See Ezekiel 36:26.

8. David Platt, "Boldness: Do We Want Him?" Sermon, The Church at Brook Hills, Birmingham, AL, July 15, 2007, http://www.radical.net/ files/uploads/Lifeline_TS2_Web.pdf. Accessed May 19, 2016.

9. R. Kent Hughes, *John: That You May Believe*, Preaching the Word (Wheaton, IL: Crossway Books, 1999), 354.

10. Dietrich Bonhoeffer, *Life Together: The Classic Exploration of Christian in Community* (New York: HarperOne, 2009), 111.

11. Leon Morris, *The Gospel According to Matthew*, The Pillar New Testament Commentary (Grand Rapids, MI; Leicester, England: Wm. B. Eerdmans Publishing Co.; InterVarsity Press, 1992), 58–59.

12. John MacArthur, *Matthew 1–7* (Chicago: Moody Publishers, 1985), 72.

13. See Matthew 25:46.

14. Mike Carter, "Student punished for Preaching Sues Everett School District," www.seattletimes.com/seattle-news/student-punished-for-preaching-sues-everett-school-district. Accessed January 21, 2017.

15. R. Kent Hughes, *Romans: Righteousness from Heaven,* Preaching the Word (Wheaton, IL: Crossway Books, 1991), 25.

16. C. J. Ellicott, *A Bible Commentary for English Readers,* http://biblehub.com/commentaries/1_corinthians/2-2.htm. Accessed December 14, 2016.

17. James Montgomery Boice, *Romans: Justification by Faith,* vol. 1 (Grand Rapids, MI: Baker Book House, 1991), 112.

18. John MacArthur, "The only way you're living your best life now is if you're going to hell." October 17, 2013, 1:26 p.m. Tweet.

19. Washoe (chimpanzee), [Wikipedia] https://en.wikipedia.org/wiki/Washoe_(chimpanzee). Accessed December 19, 2016.

20. Leon Morris, *The Epistle to the Romans,* The Pillar New Testament Commentary (Grand Rapids, MI: Wm. B. Eerdmans Publishing Co, 1988), 261.

21. Theo Balcomb, *A Promise Unfulfilled: 1962 MLK Speech Recording Is Discovered,* http://www.npr.org/2014/01/20/264226759/a-promise-unfulfilled-1962-mlk-speech-recording-is-discovered. Accessed January 18, 2017.

22. Warren W. Wiersbe, *Wiersbe's Expository Outlines on the New Testament* (Wheaton, IL: Victor Books, 1992), 384.

23. Dr. Glen E. Clifton, *Being "In Christ" We Have Victroy* (Grand Rapids, MI: WestBow Press, 2012), 197.

24. Basil Miller, *Praying Hyde: Missionary to India* (Greenville, SC: Ambassador Books, 2008), 1.

25. R. Kent Hughes, *Philippians: The Fellowship of the Gospel,* Preaching the Word (Wheaton, IL: Crossway Books, 2007), 40.

26. See 1 Kings 3:16–28.

27. Walter Bauer, *A Greek-English Lexicon of the New Testament and Other Early Christian Literature Third Edition* (Chicago, IL: University of Chicago Press, 2000), 282.

28. Commentary on Philippians 1:9–11, http://www.preceptaustin.org. Accessed January 21, 2017.

29. Charles Duhigg, *The Power of Habit* (New York: Random House, 2012), 97–126.

30. Joseph Norris "Influence," http://www.inspirationalstories.com/poems/influence-joseph-norris-poem. Accessed November 20, 2016.

31. S. Lewis Johnson, "Studies in the Epistle to the Colossians, Part I," *Bibliotheca Sacra* (Dallas Theological Seminary, vol. 118, #472, Oct. 61), 340.

32. John MacArthur, *Colossians and Philemon* (Chicago: Moody Publishers, 1992), 29.

33. Kurt Eichenwald, "The Bible: So Misunderstood It's a Sin," *Newsweek* (January 2, 2014), http://www.newsweek.com/2015/01/02/thats-not-what-bible-says-294018.html. Accessed September 16, 2015.

34. Warren W. Wiersbe, *Be Complete (Colossians): Become the Whole Person God Intends You to Be (The Be Series Commentary),* new ed. (Colorado Springs, CO: David C. Cook, 2008), 46.

35. Martin Luther, "A Mighty Fortress Is Our God," published 1531, https://en.wikipedia.org/wiki/A_Mighty_Fortress_Is_Our_God. Accessed January 10, 2017.

36. Chagigah 9b, http://www.sefaria.org/Chagigah.9b?lang=bi. Accessed January 10, 2017.

37. Shmuel Safrai, "Education and the Study of the Torah," *The Jewish People of the First Century,* Volume Two, (Philadelphia, PA: Fortress, 1976), 945–70.

38. David Haddad, *Ma'aseh Avos* (Jerusalem, Israel: Feldheim Publishing, 2007), 188.

39. Neil Postman, *Amusing Ourselves to Death: Public Discourse in the Age of Show Business*, 20th ed. (New York: Penguin Books, 2006), 1.

40. Rick Gillis, *The Real Secret to Finding a Job? Make Me Money or Save Me Money!* (Bloomington, IN: Trafford Publishing, 2009), 101.

41. Kathleen Welton, ed., *The Little Book of Gratitude Quotes* (Chicago, IL: 2011), 74.

42. John R. Rice, *The Sword Book of Treasures* (Murfreesboro, TN: The Sword of the Lord Publishers, 1946), 183.

43. Simon Guillebaud, *More than Conquerors* (Oxford, UK: Monarch Books, 2006), 173–74.

44. Walter Wilson, *The Yielded Life*, http://www.dtminc.org/They %20Found%20The%20Secret /They% 20Found%20the%20 Secret%20For%20Today%20-%209%20-%20Dr.%20 Walter%20Wilson.pdf.Accessed February 10, 2016.

45. I devoted two chapters in my book, *Firmly Planted,* defusing this argument.

46. Timothy George, *Faithful Witness: The Life and Mission of William Carey* (Downers Grove, IL: InterVarsity Press, 1992), 93.

47. See 2 Timothy 4:7.

48. Walter Kaufmann, ed., *The Portable Nietzsche* (New York: Penguin Group, 1982), 570.

49. This is a quote often attributed to C. S. Lewis, though we have no documented reference of him saying it. Rick Warren wrote a version of this quote in *The Purpose-Driven Life* (Grand Rapids, MI: Zondervan, 2002), 148.

50. Timothy George, *Galatians*, vol. 30, The New American Commentary (Nashville: Broadman & Holman Publishers, 1994), 400.

51. John Stott, *Only One Way: The Message of Galatians* (Downers Grove, IL: InterVarsity Press, 1978), 156.

52. Howard and Geraldine Taylor, *Hudson Taylor's Spiritual Secret* (Peabody, MA: Hendrickson, 2008), 131.

53. See Hebrews 9:25–26, 28; 10:9, 12, 14.

ABOUT THE AUTHOR

Robby Gallaty is the senior pastor of Long Hollow Baptist Church in Hendersonville, Tennessee. He was radically saved out of a life of drug addiction on November 12, 2002. In 2008, he began Replicate Ministries to equip and train men and women to be disciples who make disciples. He is also the author of *Creating An Atmosphere to Hear God Speak* (2009), *Unashamed: Taking a Radical Stand for Christ* (2010), *Growing Up: How to Be a Disciple Who Makes Disciples* (2013), *Firmly Planted: How to Cultivate a Faith Rooted in Christ* (2015), *Rediscovering Discipleship: Making Jesus's Final Words Our First Work* (2015), *MARCS of a Disciple* (2016), *The Forgotten Jesus: Why Western Christians Should Follow an Eastern Rabbi* (2017), *Recovered* (2019), and *Replicate* (2020).

Develop a discipleship plan

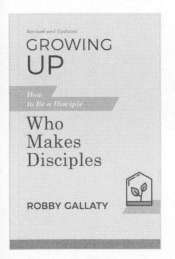

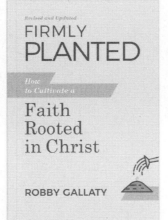

AVAILABLE
WHERE BOOKS
ARE SOLD.

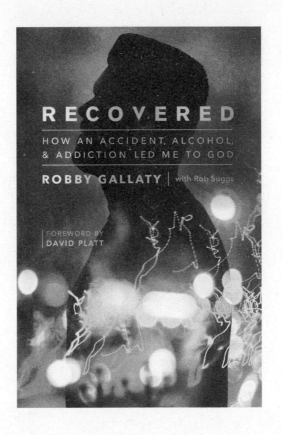